Problem solving

The School Mathematics Project

CAMBRIDGE
UNIVERSITY PRESS

Main authors   Stan Dolan
                      Tim Everton
                      Ron Haydock
                      Tom Patton
                      Jeff Searle

Team leader   Ron Haydock

Project director Stan Dolan

Initial work on various case studies was carried out by members of the Spode Group. Many others have helped with advice and criticism.

The School Mathematics Project would like to acknowledge the prior work on mathematical modelling by Mechanics in Action, Northern Ireland Further Mathematics Scheme and the Open University.

The authors would like to give special thanks to Ann White for her help in producing the trial edition and in preparing this book for publication.

The publishers would like to thank the following for supplying photographs:

Front cover – John Stuart/The Image Bank;
page 19 – George East/Science Photo Library;
page 27 – Paul Felix;
page 29 – Alan L. Edwards;
page 83 – Sarah Lightfoot.

Cartoons by Tony Hall

Published by the Press Syndicate of the University of Cambridge
The Pitt Building, Trumpington Street, Cambridge CB2 1RP
40 West 20th Street, New York, NY 10011–4211, USA
10 Stamford Road, Oakleigh, Melbourne 3166, Australia

© Cambridge University Press 1991

First published 1991
Third printing 1994

Produced by Gecko Limited, Bicester, Oxon.

Cover design by Iguana Creative Design

Printed in Great Britain at the University Press, Cambridge

British Library cataloguing in publication data

16–19 mathematics.
Problem-solving. Pupil's text
1. Mathematics. Problem-solving
I. School Mathematics Project
510

ISBN 0 521 38844 9 paperback

Contents

TYNEMOUTH COLLEGE
MATHEMATICS

1 Mathematical enquiries

1.1 Introduction

In this book we try to unravel some of the processes of mathematical activity. However, considerable independence of thought is necessary if you are to be able to tackle unfamiliar problems with confidence. To develop an investigative attitude to mathematics you must always pursue your own ideas!

To start you off, exercise 1 contains three problems which may be attempted in any order. As you work through them note the strategies you use – what methods you have of setting out to crack an unfamiliar puzzle or investigating a new situation. The problems will be referred to later, so keep a record of your solutions. All the extensions should be attempted but they are quite demanding and you should feel satisfied if you manage just one in depth.

It may be helpful to work with a small group of fellow students on some stages of discussion or investigation. It is important that you should then write an individual account and attempt to extend the work on your own.

EXERCISE 1

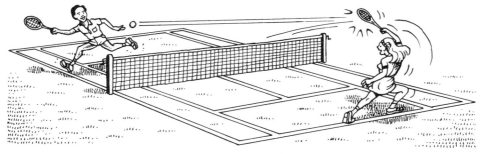

1   Eleven players enter for a singles knockout tennis tournament. The two organisers decide not to attempt any seeding but to pair at random. They disagree about byes; Joe wants all byes to be in the first round but Susan says that in each round as many players as possible should be involved.

Make a full analysis of the two suggestions, including in each case:

(a) the number of byes,   (b) the number of rounds,
(c) the total number of matches played.

Extend your investigation by considering numbers other than 11.

4

2   Think of a three-digit number, i.e. a whole number between 100 and 999. Reverse its digits and find the difference between the 'reversed' number and the original number. Check that it is a multiple of 99. Try one or two more examples.

Now try following the same procedure with numbers with two, four and five digits. Do you get a similar result?

Extend your investigation so that you can make and explain a general statement about your findings.

3   'Everybody knows' that equilateral triangles and squares will tessellate. What exactly is meant by this?

Show that:

(a) a tessellation can be made using any parallelogram,

(b) a tessellation can be made using any triangle,

(c) no tessellation can be made using a regular pentagon.

Extend your investigation by considering other shapes. Is there **any** pentagon which will tessellate? Can **all** quadrilaterals tessellate?

1.2 Starting an enquiry

In attempting the problems of exercise 1 you may have felt in turn frustrated, bored, then interested and (it is hoped) finally satisfied that you had reached a pretty good understanding. In this chapter and the next, the mathematical activities which accompanied these various emotions are analysed. A vocabulary is introduced which you should use in future solutions.

The analysis will not be exhaustive; for example there is no specific mention of the skill of using iterative techniques. This is because the text concentrates on features common to many problems. Of course, you can use any method you like to solve problems. The analysis of processes is there to help, not to constrain.

You should read with pencil and notebook at the ready; to check the various assertions made, work through the exercises and make notes. For each process a brief explanation is given, followed by a few exercises. Do not get too carried away by these exercises: just deal with the particular process under discussion. In certain cases you will meet a problem more than once because it gives a good illustration of more than one process.

The first example illustrates the use of mathematical processes which seem to be particularly important. They are:

- investigating particular cases;
- finding patterns;
- generalising.

E X A M P L E 1

Investigate
$$1^3 + 2^3 =$$
$$1^3 + 2^3 + 3^3 =$$
$$1^3 + 2^3 + 3^3 + 4^3 =$$

S O L U T I O N

A first reaction might be to work out these **particular cases** and **look for a pattern**. You might then predict the next line in the sequence.

$$1^3 + 2^3 + 3^3 + 4^3 + 5^3 =$$

> What general **pattern** is suggested by the numbers obtained on the right-hand side?

Investigating further **particular cases** seems to confirm the general pattern:

$$1^3 + 2^3 + 3^3 + 4^3 + 5^3 \quad\;\; = 225 = 15^2$$
$$1^3 + 2^3 + 3^3 + 4^3 + 5^3 + 6^3 = 441 = 21^2$$

> Can you refine the **pattern** so that there is some easy way of predicting what the square number will be for each particular case?

You need to look for a connection between the numbers on the left-hand side and the resulting square number on the right-hand side.

$$1 + 2 \qquad\qquad\qquad = \;\; 3$$
$$1 + 2 + 3 \qquad\qquad\; = \;\; 6$$
$$1 + 2 + 3 + 4 \qquad\; = 10$$
$$1 + 2 + 3 + 4 + 5 \quad\; = 15$$
$$1 + 2 + 3 + 4 + 5 + 6 = 21$$

> Explain the **pattern** of the original results in words.

In symbols, the pattern can be expressed as the **generalisation**

$$1^3 + 2^3 + 3^3 + \ldots + n^3 = (1 + 2 + 3 + \ldots + n)^2$$

It still remains to verify or prove that this general result holds for all possible particular cases. The important process of proof is discussed later.

The two processes of **investigating particular cases** and **finding patterns** both appear in this example but in no obviously systematic way. The processes are like tools used as and when the need arises. For the problem just considered, the process of mathematical enquiry has appeared to be:

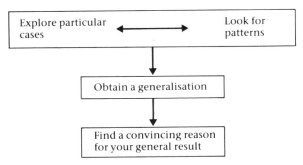

You can now go on to analyse these and other processes in more detail.

1.3 **Particular cases**

Often a problem asks for a general result, for example the number of byes in a tournament with n players. If no solution immediately suggests itself then you might decide to experiment with particular values of n. In the tennis tournament problem of exercise 1, you were invited to start with $n = 11$ and then try other particular cases. Perhaps you tried the case of 12 players, or a number chosen at random. Similarly, in the tessellation problem, a particular kind of quadrilateral – a parallelogram – was considered initially. Although none of these particular cases may have led directly to a general solution they can give you a hint on how to approach the general case.

It is often (though not always) best to consider particular cases methodically in some sort of order. Very often the smallest possible case is important but sometimes particular cases are chosen for other reasons.

> Which values of n are especially important particular cases in the tournament problem?

EXERCISE 2

1 In discussing the solution of equations of the form

$$x^3 + ax + b = 0$$

for various values of a and b, which particular values might you dispose of before treating the general case?

2 In teaching a young child how to find the area of a triangle, which special kind of triangle would you first consider?

3 In sketching the graph of $y = x + \dfrac{1}{x}$, which particular values of x would you first consider?

4 (a) Find a particular set of values of the numbers a, b, c, d, e and f for which the simultaneous equations

$$ax + by = c$$
$$dx + ey = f$$

have no solutions in x and y.

(b) Find another set for which the equations have an infinity of solutions.

1.4 **Forming patterns**

In original mathematical investigations, guesswork can loom large, though this is not always apparent in the final written account. At this level a guess is often given the more respectable name of **conjecture**; thus: conjecture – knockout tournaments with 2^n players have no byes. If this is not immediately obvious you can verify it in **particular cases** by drawing up tournament tables for (1, 2,) 4, 8, 16, . . . players.

Because a conjecture can be verified for some particular values of n it is not necessarily true for all values of n. Having shown the results to be true in a few cases you should then try to give a convincing argument that the conjecture is true for **all** possible values of n; that is, you need to prove the result. The process of proof will be discussed in chapter 4.

The patterns formed in your investigations need not be of numbers; they may be actual geometrical patterns, such as you made in answering the tessellation problem of exercise 1. Such patterns can give rise to further interesting problems.

Use conjecture and pattern-spotting to investigate:

$(1 \times 2 \times 3 \times 4) + 1 =$
$(2 \times 3 \times 4 \times 5) + 1 =$
$(3 \times 4 \times 5 \times 6) + 1 =$

. . .

EXERCISE 3

1 From your investigation of the discussion point above, find consecutive integers a, b, c and d such that $(a \times b \times c \times d) + 1 = 43681$.

2 The first seven terms of the Fibonacci sequence are 1, 1, 2, 3, 5, 8, 13.

(a) What are the next two terms?

(b) Continue the sequence

$2^2 = (3 \times 1) + 1, \quad 3^2 = (5 \times 2) - 1, \quad 5^2 = (8 \times 3) + 1, \ldots$

(c) The 3rd, 6th, 9th, 12th, . . . terms are all even. List the 4th, 8th, 12th, . . . terms. What do you notice?

(d) Make a conjecture about the 5th, 10th, 15th, . . . terms and check it by working them out.

1.5 Generalisation

You will recall that the triangular numbers are

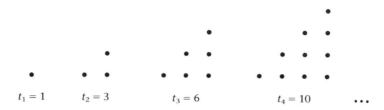

$t_1 = 1$ $t_2 = 3$ $t_3 = 6$ $t_4 = 10$ ...

and the square numbers are even more familiar:

$s_1 = 1$ $s_2 = 4$ $s_3 = 9$ $s_4 = 16$ ...

(a) Express s_3 as the sum of two triangular numbers.

(b) Express s_4 as the sum of two triangular numbers.

(c) Express s_n as the sum of two triangular numbers.

Your solution for s_n is a generalisation of which your solutions for s_3 and s_4 are particular cases.

Very often the aim of an investigation is to arrive at a general result, commonly (though not always) expressed in a formula. You may have had the satisfaction of finding that in a knockout competition with n players the minimum number of byes, number of rounds and number of matches played can all be given by formulas.

The statement 'no tessellation is possible using only a regular polygon with more than six sides' contains no formula but, being about a whole class of objects, is a generalisation.

EXERCISE 4

1   Generalise on this sequence of equations

$$1 = 1$$
$$1 + 3 = 4$$
$$1 + 3 + 5 = 9$$
$$1 + 3 + 5 + 7 = 16$$

(a) in symbols,   (b) in words.

2   The sum of two consecutive odd numbers is divisible by 4.

(a) Can you make similar statements about the sum of three consecutive odd numbers and of four consecutive odd numbers?

(b) Generalise your findings.

3   How many diagonals has a quadrilateral? A pentagon? A hexagon? A polygon with n sides?

4   (a) Of all triangles of equal perimeter, the equilateral triangle has the greatest area.

(b) Of all quadrilaterals of equal perimeter, the square has the greatest area.

Make a general statement of which (a) and (b) are particular cases.

After working through this chapter you should:

1   feel confident about starting a mathematical enquiry;

2   be ready to adopt an investigative attitude to mathematics;

3   be familiar with the use and meaning of the terms: particular cases, conjecture and generalisation;

4   have experience of problem-solving which will be of use in later chapters.

2 Organising your work

2.1 Notation and symbols

Organising your work can be very important in rendering a problem manageable – and its solution readable! In this chapter we shall consider the processes of choosing a notation, classifying and tabulation.

The choice of notation in problem-solving is often routine. In the tennis tournament problem of chapter 1 you probably used the standard tournament table.

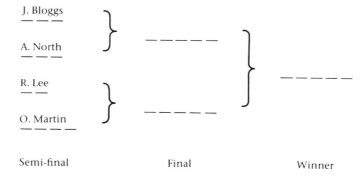

J. Bloggs

A. North

R. Lee

O. Martin

Semi-final   Final   Winner

In the digit-reversing problem of chapter 1 you probably used letters to represent the digits of a general three-digit number, the number looking like ABC having the value $100A + 10B + C$. This would have allowed you to tackle the problem algebraically.

How good are you at describing objects or giving clear directions without using a street plan?

Suppose you have to describe a diagram, such as the one below, over the telephone. How could you do it?

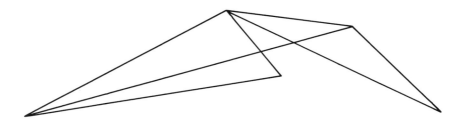

EXERCISE 1

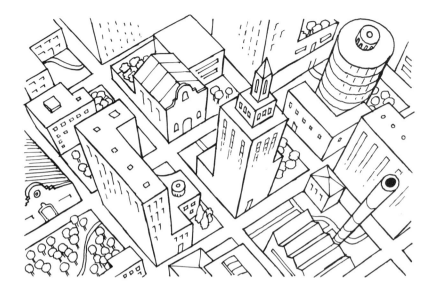

1   A journey in a US city is described by the notation R S S R S L, where

R means turn right
S means go straight on   } at the next intersection.
L means turn left

How would you describe the inverse (return) journey?

2   Think of two methods of describing a particular move in a game of 'noughts and crosses'.

3   The eight numbers 7, 8, 9, 10, 11, 12, 13, 14 can be divided into two sets of four such that the sums of the squares are equal:

$$7^2 + 10^2 + 12^2 + 13^2 = 8^2 + 9^2 + 11^2 + 14^2.$$

Is a similar statement true for other sets of eight consecutive numbers?

4   Three tumblers are arranged with just one upside-down.

Take any pair and turn them over, and continue doing this, a pair at a time, in an effort to finish with all three right way up. Invent a simple notation to explain why this is impossible.

2.2 Classifying

Sometimes an investigation is simplified if you deal with separate classes one at a time. In the digit-reversing problem of chapter 1, the class of numbers with an odd number of digits behaves differently from that with an even number of digits. An important class in the tessellation problem of chapter 1 is that of pentagons with a pair of parallel sides.

Name at least three different classes of

(a) quadrilateral,   (b) function.

EXERCISE 2

1 Name at least three different classes of

(a) angle,   (b) triangle,   (c) solid shape.

2 A strategy for the game of noughts and crosses hinges on the first move made. How many essentially different first moves are possible?

3 Which classes of quadrilateral have exactly two lines of symmetry?

4 By classifying the integers a and b as being odd or even and by considering the different combinations, show that the equation

$$a^2 + b^2 = 4c + 3$$

has no solution in integers a, b and c.

5 Your friend has a pack of eight cards and invites you to choose one at random.

He then asks three questions to which you answer 'yes' or 'no', after which he identifies the card chosen. It later turns out that he can always do this by asking the same three questions, in the same order. What might the questions be?

2.3 Tabulation

You sometimes explore particular cases in a more or less haphazard way as you feel your way into an investigation. To make progress you then need to display your findings in a more orderly fashion. At this stage a table may suggest a way ahead. Tables are important, too, in communicating information clearly to a reader of your work. For both these reasons, in solving the tennis tournament problem you may have felt the need to draw up a table like this.

No. of players	1	2	3	4	. . .
No. of byes	0	0	1	0	. . .
No. of rounds	0	1	2	2	. . .
No. of matches	0	1	2	3	. . .

TASKSHEET 1 OR 1E — Tables of differences (pages 17 and 18)

Though there are other kinds of table, of properties of shapes for example, a table is often useful when building up a sequence of numbers. In trying to find the pattern in a sequence, a **table of differences** sometimes helps. Consider the problem: what is the greatest number of points of intersection given by n lines? Starting with small values of n you can quickly draw up a table.

No. of lines	1	2	3	4	5
No. of points	0	1	3	6	10

Perhaps you do not remember the sequence in the second line. Or perhaps you vaguely recognise the triangular numbers but do not find this particularly helpful. But if you subtract each number from the one on its right, the pattern becomes clear.

$$0 \underset{\downarrow}{\top} 1 \underset{\downarrow}{\top} 3 \underset{\downarrow}{\top} 6 \underset{\downarrow}{\top} 10$$

First differences   1   2   3   4

This enables you to extend the table easily – the next 'first difference' is probably 5, so the next entry above will be 15, and so on. As a result the problem is replaced by a much simpler one; the number required appears to be

$$1 + 2 + 3 + \ldots + (n - 1)$$

EXERCISE 3

1 Make a table showing the number of diagonals of an *n*-sided polygon for values of *n* from 3 to 6. By finding first differences, conjecture the number of diagonals of a decagon. Check your conjecture.

2 Devise a table showing the properties of bilateral and rotational symmetry for parallelograms, rhombi, rectangles, kites and squares.

3

n	1	2	3	4	5
$r(n)$	1	2	2	3	3
$s(n)$	1	2	3	5	8

In the table, $r(n)$ is the number of ways of representing the number *n* as a sum, using only the terms 1 and 2, the order of the terms not being significant, for example

$$4 = 1 + 1 + 1 + 1 = 1 + 1 + 2 = 2 + 2$$

$s(n)$ is the number of ways when the order is significant, for example

$$4 = 1 + 1 + 1 + 1 = 1 + 1 + 2 = 1 + 2 + 1 = 2 + 1 + 1 = 2 + 2$$

Check the entries in the table, find $r(6)$ and $s(6)$, and conjecture a formula for $r(n)$ and a rule for generating the sequence $s(n)$.

After working through this chapter you should:

1 appreciate the need for orderly procedures and presentation;

2 be familiar with the use and meaning of the terms classification and tabulation;

3 know how to use a table of differences;

4 be able to find the degree of the polynomial generating a given sequence.

Tables of differences

To find the sequence generated by the quadratic expression

$$2n^2 - n + 3$$

you can calculate its value for $n = 1, 2, 3, \ldots$ to obtain

4, 9, 18, 31, 48, . . .

The **first differences** are found by subtracting each term from the one to its right.

4 9 18 31 48 . . .
   5   9   13   17 . . .

The process may be repeated to find **second differences**.

5 9 13 17 . . .
  4 4   4 . . .

You will see that the **third differences** would all be zero.

1 Choose another quadratic sequence, i.e. one generated by an expression of the form

$$an^2 + bn + c$$

where a, b and c are integers. Find first and second differences.

2 Use a cubic sequence, generated by an expression of the form

$$an^3 + bn^2 + cn + d$$

and find first, second and third differences.

3 Use the method of differences to make a conjecture about the sequence

$-1, -6, 3, 68, 255, 654, 1379, \ldots$

Tables of differences

To find the sequence generated by the quadratic expression

$$2n^2 - n + 3$$

you can calculate its value for $n = 1, 2, 3, \ldots$ to obtain

$$4, 9, 18, 31, 48, \ldots$$

The **first differences** are found by subtracting each term from the one to its right.

$$4 \;\; 9 \;\; 18 \;\; 31 \;\; 48 \ldots$$
$$5 \quad 9 \quad 13 \quad 17 \ldots$$

The process may be repeated to find **second differences**.

$$5 \;\; 9 \;\; 13 \;\; 17 \ldots$$
$$4 \quad 4 \quad 4 \ldots$$

You will see that the **third differences** would all be zero.

1 Choose another quadratic sequence, i.e. one generated by an expression of the form

$$an^2 + bn + c$$

where a, b and c are integers. Find first and second differences.

2 Generate a cubic sequence, giving at least six terms, using an expression of the form

$$an^3 + bn^2 + cn + d$$

and find first, second and third differences.

3 Find the tables of differences given by sequences generated by the expressions:

(a) n (b) n^2 (c) n^3 (d) n^4

4 If the fifth differences given by a sequence are all 30, how do you think the sequence was generated? (Answer in as much detail as you can.)

3 Mathematical modelling

3.1 Solar eclipses

Partial and total eclipses of the sun have long both terrified and fascinated humanity. We now know that an eclipse occurs when the earth, moon and sun are in a straight line with the moon between the earth and the sun.

During a total eclipse, all that is visible of the sun is a bright ring (called the corona) surrounding a black disc (the moon). The diagram below shows successive stages in a total eclipse of the sun. The difference in apparent size of the discs representing the sun and moon is exaggerated.

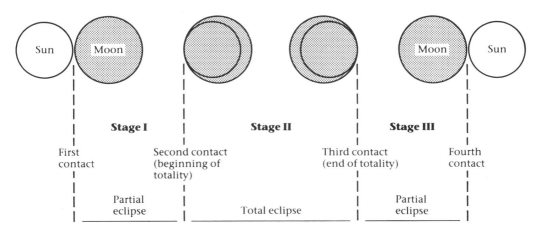

The period of total eclipse is in stage II. During stages I and III, a partial eclipse is observed.

The total eclipse is only seen on a narrow band of the earth's surface known as the zone of totality or the umbra.

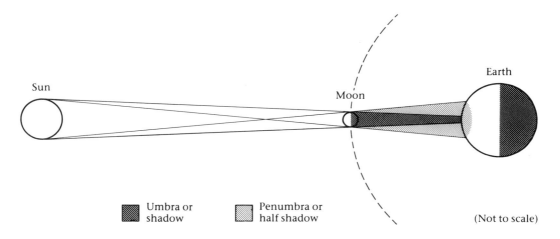

| Umbra or shadow | | Penumbra or half shadow | (Not to scale) |

To an observer standing in the penumbra, the moon passes in front of the sun but never completely obscures it and only a partial eclipse is observed.

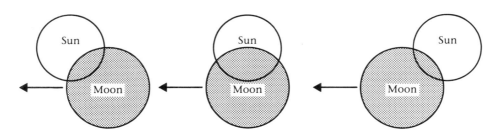

The last total eclipse visible from Britain was in 1927 and the next one is due in 1999!

Mathematics has a vital role to play in our attempts to explain and understand events we observe in the world. Mathematical tools enable us to predict that there **will** be a total eclipse in 1999, to determine its duration and to pick the best observation point.

The following problem is much easier to state than to solve! It is best tackled as a group exercise.

> How long does a total eclipse last?

Determining the duration of a total eclipse involves a complex problem-solving process. Some of the stages in this process are examined in the next section.

3.2 Modelling processes

Various examples of mathematical modelling can be found in other units of the *16–19 Mathematics* course. Modelling is concerned with using pure mathematical techniques and processes to solve 'real' problems. There are several important stages concerned with deciding what mathematical techniques need to be applied and making sense of the answers obtained. In attempting to solve 'real' problems, we go from the real world into the theoretical world of mathematics and back again.

The process of modelling can be represented by the following modelling loop.

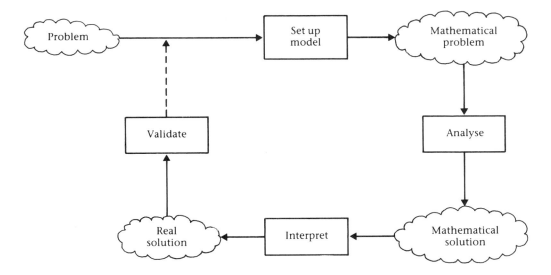

Set up model   Define the real problem.
Formulate the mathematical problem. (This often involves deciding what variables are relevant and what connecting relationships can be assumed.)

Analyse   Solve the mathematical problem.

Interpret   Interpret the solution in real terms.

Validate   Compare the solution with reality. If the solution does not compare well with reality, then you must go around the loop again, refining the model.

Consider your solution to the total eclipse problem. Try to identify the four stages of the modelling process described above.

SET UP MODEL

The stage of setting up a model is at the heart of the mathematical modelling process. It is important to choose suitable simplifying assumptions which preserve the key features of the real situation but which avoid an unnecessarily complicated model. Essentially, there are two key stages in setting up a model.

- Decide on the relevant variables, keeping your list as short and simple as possible.

- Look for relations connecting the variables on your list.

For the total eclipse problem, initial models were chosen in which the relevant variables were the distances on the diagram below, together with the orbital speed of the moon and time of the eclipse.

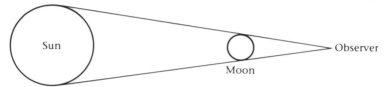

In this case, a relationship between the distances can be obtained from the diagram and a further relationship is

distance = speed × time

ANALYSE

For the eclipse problem a further simplification was made, producing the similar triangles shown below.

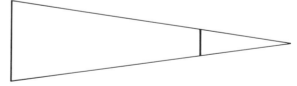

The mathematical analysis was then simply the use of similar triangles, followed later by a use of the distance–speed relationship.

INTERPRET

When modelling 'real' problems it is important to remember that 'real' answers are required. If you are trying to estimate the annual cost of running the family car, then an answer such as £4000 is required and not an algebraic formula.

An analysis of the initial eclipse model had a very simple interpretation – total eclipses cannot occur!

VALIDATE

It will be possible to check the solutions to many problems by direct comparison with reality.

You know that total eclipses do occur and so the initial model needed refining. Even after two successive refinements the eclipse model still predicted a much shorter eclipse than can actually occur.

> The acid test of a model is always how well it represents reality but, generally, over-elaboration should be avoided.
>
> Normally a model will need improvement and you will have to go round the loop in the flow chart a second or even a third time. At some point, however, the model will be judged to be good enough and you stop.

Mathematical modelling occurs when solving pure problems as well as 'real' ones.

EXAMPLE 1

The product of the ages of Ann and Mike is 300. Find their ages if Ann is 20 years older than Mike.

SOLUTION

Let Mike be m years old; then Ann is $m + 20$ years old.

Set up model   Appropriate notation is introduced for the variables.

$m(m + 20) = 300$

Relationships are listed.

$\Rightarrow \quad m^2 + 20m - 300 = 0$
$\Rightarrow \quad (m + 30)(m - 10) = 0$
$\Rightarrow \quad m = -30 \text{ or } 10$

Analyse   The standard method of solving a quadratic equation by factorisation is applied.

m cannot be -30 and so $m = 10$.

Mike is 10 and Ann is 30.

Interpret/validate   The two mathematical solutions yield only one 'real' solution. This solution is then stated in everyday language.

3.3 Modelling exercises

You should select one or two of the problems introduced on the following tasksheets. In each case you should apply the stages of mathematical modelling to obtain a **practical** solution.

TASKSHEETS

1 – Reading age (page 25)
2 – Wallpapering guide (page 26)
3 – Fencing (page 27)
4 – Journeys (page 28)
5 – Sports day (group project) (page 29)
6 – Miscellany (page 30)

After working through this chapter you should be able to recognise and apply the following stages in the modelling process:

set up model: define the real problem, decide which variables are relevant, decide what relationships can be assumed;

analyse: solve the mathematical problem;

interpret: interpret the solution in real terms;

validate: compare the solution with reality, modify your model as necessary.

Reading age

There are a number of indices for finding the reading ages of different kinds of text.

SIMPLICITY FORMULA

$$25 - 15p$$

where p is the proportion of words of one syllable.

FOG INDEX

$$\frac{2}{5}\left(\frac{A}{n} + \frac{100L}{A}\right)$$

where A is the number of words, n the number of sentences and L the number of long words (with three or more syllables).

SMOG FORMULA

$$8 + \sqrt{p}$$

where p is the number of words with three or more syllables in 30 sentences.

In general, each formula has a limited range of validity. For example, the Smog formula is clearly not applicable to books for 5 and 6 year olds.

For a chosen type of article or book, design a method of assessing reading age. Use it to compare several examples and decide how you would validate your method.

Wallpapering guide

1 Suppose you have decided to redecorate your bedroom. How many rolls of wallpaper will you need?

(a) Write out a list of the relevant variables.

(b) Write down any simplifying assumptions that can be made and shorten your list of variables where appropriate.

(c) What calculations do you need to make to answer the original problem?

2 Generalise your solution to question 1. You should aim to obtain a simple guide such as a formula:

$$\frac{\text{Height (metres)} \times \text{Perimeter (metres)}}{5}$$

or perhaps a table:

Height (metres)	Perimeter (metres)			
	10	14	18	22
2.00–2.10	5	6	8	10
...	...	...	...	...

Fencing

The main work of a fencing contractor is to put up lengths of timber fencing, with five rails and supporting posts at 2 metre intervals.

The contractor has consulted you to find a simple way of estimating for fencing work.

1   Suppose that the length to be fenced is 40 m. Find the cost of suitable railing and posts and decide an appropriate allowance for labour. Hence make a first estimate for the work.

2   Refine your model to take into account details overlooked in the first estimate.

3   Generalise the model, obtaining a method for calculating the cost of erecting any such fence.

4   Make sure that the contractor has a **simple** means of estimating for work.

Journeys

You have an appointment at 9:15 a.m. In order to get there you will travel by car from your home. Obviously you wish the journey to be as straightforward and economical as possible.

What factors will you need to consider in determining a straightforward and economical route?

In order to answer this question, you should choose a specific destination in an area with which you are familiar.

Choose a destination which:

(a) will be at least one hour's journey-time from your home;

(b) can be reached by at least three alternative routes or parts of routes.

Write a report which gives the route you would take and the time at which you would leave. Include your reasons for choosing this route in preference to others.

Sports day

This tasksheet is suitable for a group project.

Select a field in the vicinity of your school or home as a prospective sports ground.

Carry out a survey or use a large scale map to make a scale plan of the field.

Find the best way of marking out the field for athletic competitions to include:

* 100 m, 200 m and 400 m races,
* long jump and high jump,
* discus, hammer and javelin throwing,
* shot putting.

On your plan, include arrangements for competitors, judges and spectators.

Miscellany

1 Consider the annual costs of running the family car.

(a) Write out a list of the relevant variables.

(b) Write down any important simplifying assumptions.

(c) Set up a relation connecting the total annual costs with other relevant variables, including the distance travelled annually.

2 Determine how many molecules from the dying breath of Julius Caesar you inhale with each breath.

3 Suppose you have to design a £1 book of stamps for the Post Office, to cater for both first and second class post.

(a) What data would you require?

(b) Write down the relevant variables and the relationships between them.

(c) Decide on a suitable design and justify your decision.

4 Life is full of decision-making but it is often difficult to make choices on purely rational grounds. How good are you at decision-making? Carefully evaluate the options connected with some major choice people have to make in their lives. For example:

• Is going to university a sound **financial** investment?

• Is it better to buy or rent your home?

4 Completing investigations

4.1 Counter-example

Sometimes conjectures are not true, despite a good deal of evidence. For example, suppose that a friend, having tried many particular pentagons, is convinced that no pentagon will tessellate. To refute this generalisation, all you have to do is produce a single counter-example.

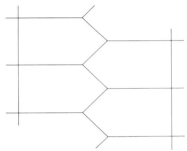

This means that disproof is often a very short and simple matter (provided that you have the counter-example to hand!), whereas proof is such a complicated business that whole books can be written about it.

EXERCISE 1

1   Disprove, by finding a suitable counter-example, the statement

$$x^2 > y^2 \Rightarrow x > y$$

2   If two lines are perpendicular to a third line then they must be parallel to each other – true or false?

3   $1 = 0^2 + 1^2, \quad 5 = 1^2 + 2^2, \quad 9 = 0^2 + 3^2 \quad \ldots, 97 = 4^2 + 9^2$

All numbers of the form $(4n + 1)$ may be expressed as a sum of two squares – true or false?

4   Find the first four terms, t_1, t_2, t_3 and t_4 for the sequence defined by

$$t_n = (n - 1)(n - 2)(n - 3)(n - 4) + n$$

What might you expect t_5 to be? Is it?

4.2 Proof

In the previous section, you considered several conjectures which could be disproved by finding counter-examples.

> When you have a conjecture of your own, how can you be sure that no-one will be able to find a counter-example?

TASKSHEET 1 — Convincing reasons (page 40)

Simply spotting a pattern is not the end of a mathematical investigation. You then need **either** to look for a convincing reason for the pattern **or** to find a counter-example.

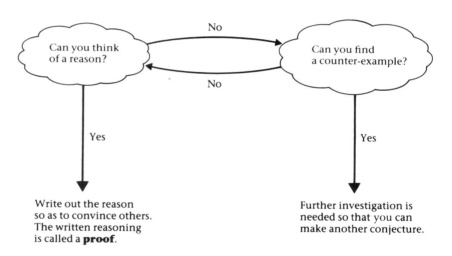

The real challenge of a mathematical investigation is to break out of the potentially endless 'no–no' cycle of not being able to find **either** a convincing reason **or** a counter–example!

> Amassing particular cases, no matter how many, does not establish a general result. To complete your investigation you must normally find convincing reasons for any patterns or results you have discovered.

E X A M P L E   1

Prove that $(1 + 2 + 3 + \ldots + n)^2 = 1^3 + 2^3 + 3^3 + \ldots + n^3$.

S O L U T I O N

Building up the left side of the equation above by adding 'shells' provides a geometrical approach.

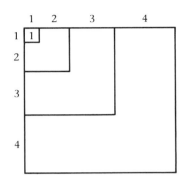

Verify that the L-shaped shells have areas 8, 27 and 64 square units respectively.

The diagram demonstrates that

$$(1 + 2 + 3 + 4)^2 = 1^3 + 2^3 + 3^3 + 4^3$$

You need to show that, in general, the kth shell has area k^3. For this, use the result

$$1 + 2 + 3 + \ldots + (k - 1) = \tfrac{1}{2}k(k - 1)$$

For instance, as you can see in the top diagram, the fourth shell has an 'inside arm' measurement of $1 + 2 + 3 = \tfrac{1}{2} \times 4 \times 3$.

The kth shell looks like this when divided into three parts.

$\tfrac{1}{2}k(k - 1)$

B

k A   C

Find areas A, B and C and show that $A + B + C = k^3$.

The area of a square of side $(1 + 2 + \ldots + n)$ is the sum of the areas of n shells. So

$$(1 + 2 + \ldots + n)^2 = 1^3 + 2^3 + \ldots + n^3$$

EXERCISE 2

1   What is wrong with the following demonstration that the area of an 8×8 square is the same as the area of a 5×13 rectangle?

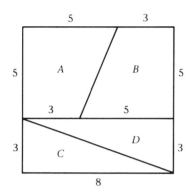

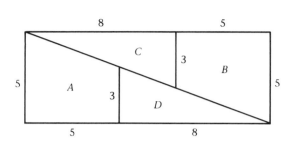

2   In chapter 2, when answering question 1 of exercise 3, you may have found that the number of diagonals of a polygon is as given in this table:

Number of sides	3	4	5	6	7	...	n
Number of diagonals	0	2	5	9	14	...	$\frac{1}{2}n(n-3)$

Complete the following reason for the last entry in the table.

'From each of the n corners, $n - 3$ diagonals can be drawn . . .'

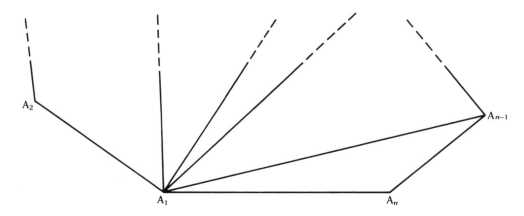

3   (See chapter 1, exercise 4, question 2.)

(a)   Prove that the sum of two consecutive odd numbers is divisible by 4.

(b)   Prove the generalisation that you made in answering question 2 of exercise 4.

4.3 **Fermat and proof**

In question 3 of exercise 1 you may have discovered that 21 cannot be expressed as the sum of two squares. The seventeenth-century amateur mathematician Pierre de Fermat studied a refinement of the conjecture that you looked at in exercise 1.

All primes of the form $(4n + 1)$ can be expressed as the sum of two squares.

Of his attempts to prove this conjecture, Fermat wrote (*Diophantus*, page 268):

'. . . when I had to prove that every prime number of the form $(4n + 1)$ is made up of two squares, I found myself in a pretty fix.'

Fermat was in the 'no–no' cycle. However,

'But at last a certain reflection many times repeated gave me the necessary light, and affirmative questions yielded to my method, with the aid of some new principles by which sheer necessity compelled me to supplement it.'

Another problem with which Fermat wrestled is known as 'Fermat's last theorem'. The problem is to prove that there are no positive integers x, y, z such that, for some integer m greater than 2,

$$x^m + y^m = z^m$$

There are certainly positive integers satisfying $x^2 + y^2 = z^2$:

$$x = 3, y = 4, z = 5 \quad \text{and} \quad x = 5, y = 12, z = 13$$

are well-known cases. Fermat's theorem is that $x^3 + y^3 = z^3$, $x^4 + y^4 = z^4$, and so on, **cannot** be solved for positive integers x, y and z.

Of this problem, Fermat wrote (*Diophantus*, page 145):

'I have discovered a truly marvellous proof of this, which however the margin is not large enough to contain.'

To date, no-one has been able to find either a complete proof of this result or a counter-example, although it has been proved for many values of m. However, attempts on this problem have stimulated many important advances in Number Theory. When you are in the 'no–no' cycle, the ideas you think of and try may be far more important than any eventual solution to the problem!

You may feel that proof is not really a part of problem-solving as such. After all, you may argue, the problem has really been solved when you reach the point of 'knowing', and proving is then no more than icing on the cake. The trouble is that you often do not 'know' until a proof has been found.

TASKSHEET 2 — Regions of a circle (page 41)

We hope that you will devise proofs, where necessary, that will stand up to your own critical examination and that of your fellow students. Ultimately a proof is 'that which carries conviction'. We hope that you will become increasingly difficult to convince and increasingly good at convincing others.

TASKSHEET 3E — Prime number formulas (page 42)

Just as there is a loop for mathematical modelling, a simplified outline for the process of solving a pure problem can also be represented by a loop:

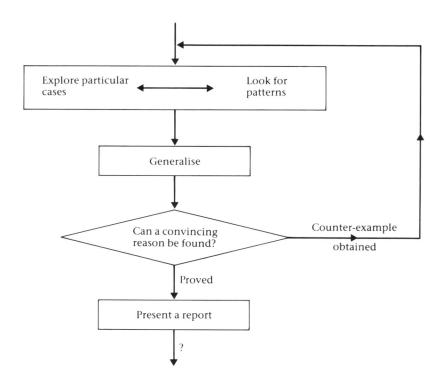

Even when you have written up your findings, the investigation may not be over . . .

4.4 Extending an investigation

Even when you are satisfied with your solution to a problem, you may find that one investigation can lead to another.

Suppose you had solved the problem of finding how many squares of various sizes are bounded by the lines in a 4 × 4 grid. You might then go on to look at what is essentially another particular case, say that of the 5 × 5 grid. This is a fairly trivial form of extension of a problem, though it might lead ultimately to a **generalisation**. On the other hand you might ask yourself the question: **what would happen if** a triangular grid had been used?

 TASKSHEET 4 OR 4E – Square and triangular grids (pages 44 and 45)

The original problem of finding the number of squares on a 4 × 4 grid can be extended in a variety of ways:

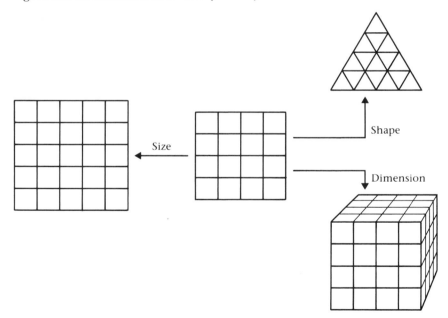

An extension into an analogous problem is more interesting when the new situation, though related, is really different from the old one.

The square and cubical grids also have a one-dimensional analogue – five equally spaced points in a straight line. So there is a chain of analogous problems.

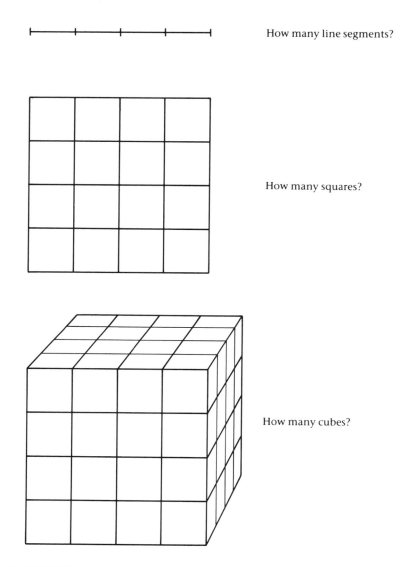

How many line segments?

How many squares?

How many cubes?

(a) Show how the answers to the three problems are analogous.

(b) In the first problem, the five points need not be in line. Use this idea to deduce the number of diagonals of a pentagon.

When tackling investigations of your own, you should be aware that all investigations have scope for extension!

After working through this chapter you should:

1   be aware that a general result cannot be established simply by considering a large number of particular cases;

2   appreciate that mathematical advances occur when mathematicians have been unable to find either a proof or a counter-example;

3   be more difficult to convince;

4   be better at convincing others by improving the standards of rigour in your arguments;

5   appreciate that all investigations have scope for extension.

Convincing reasons

1 (a) **Explain** why $2n$ is always even for all integer values of n.

   (b) Write down a number, in terms of n, which you know is odd. Explain **how** you know.

   (c) 'The sum of three consecutive odd numbers is always divisible by 3.' Check this conjecture by considering a number of cases. Write out a convincing explanation.

2 Take any two-digit number, reverse its digits and add to the original number. For example:

$$\begin{array}{r} 34 \\ +43 \\ \hline 77 \end{array} = 11 \times 7$$

A convincing explanation that the result will always be divisible by 11 might start by letting the two digits be a and b, so that the original number is $10a + b$.

   (a) Write down the value of the 'reversed' number.

   (b) Find the sum of the numbers and show that the sum **is** always divisible by 11.

   (c) Discover if the rule applies to three- or four-digit numbers. Explain your findings.

3 A neat party trick is the following rule for multiplication by 11, illustrated by $11 \times 321 = 3531$.

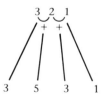

For 11×1325 you can therefore proceed by:

$$11 \times 1\overset{+}{}3\overset{+}{}2\overset{+}{}5 = 14\,575.$$

   (a) Check that this method always seems to work.

   (b) Using the method of expressing a two-digit number used in question 2 (i.e. 'ab' $= 10a + b$), explain how this method for multiplying by 11 works.

Regions of a circle

The problem is:

> How many regions are formed when n points on the circumference of a circle are joined?

It can be tackled step by step as follows:

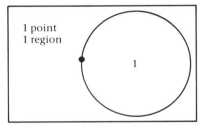

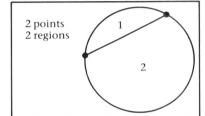

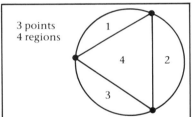

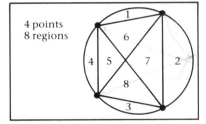

1 Tabulate this information, guess a pattern and write a general formula based on your conjecture.

2 Check your formula in the cases $n = 5$ and $n = 6$.

   You must draw the diagram for $n = 6$ **very** carefully if you are not to miscount the number of regions. To obtain the greatest number of regions for $n = 6$, you must **not** draw, for example, a regular hexagon.

3 At this stage, after a recount, your investigation will need to take a fresh direction. Extend your table up to 7 points.

4 Make a table of differences.

5 Make a final conjecture.

Prime number formulas

Many quadratic formulas generate long strings of prime numbers. The formula $n^2 - n + 41$ is a much quoted example.

First conjecture $n^2 - n + 41$ is always prime.

This is not true; for example when $n = 41$, $n^2 - n + 41 = 41^2$, which is not prime.

After trying many other expressions you might make a totally different type of conjecture.

Second conjecture   No quadratic expression in n is prime for all integral values of n.

> Write down various quadratic expressions in n, for example
>
> $$n^2 + 7n + 5, \quad n^2 - 1, \quad 3n^2 + 2$$
>
> Can you always find a value of n for which the expression is not prime?

It is likely that the more quadratic expressions you try, the more you will become convinced of the truth of the second conjecture. But, as you know, it is not sufficient simply to try lots of examples – you may miss the one example which turns out to be a counter-example!

This is the exciting phase of the solution of a mathematical problem where all sorts of ideas must be tried out as you search for either a convincing proof or a counter-example. Two attempts at proof are given below.

FIRST ATTEMPTED PROOF

The general quadratic is of the form $an^2 + bn + c$.

Putting $n = c$ gives $ac^2 + bc + c = c(ac + b + 1)$, which is not prime because it is divisible by both $ac + b + 1$ and c. Therefore no quadratic expression in n can be prime for all integral values of n.

> Check over the 'proof' above carefully. Which particular cases spoil the 'proof'?

SECOND ATTEMPTED PROOF ('BY CONTRADICTION')

Suppose $an^2 + bn + c$ to be prime for all integers n. In particular, for $n = 1$, $a + b + c$ must be a prime. Let $a + b + c = p$.

For $n = 1 + p$,

$$an^2 + bn + c = a(p + 1)^2 + b(p + 1) + c$$
$$= ap^2 + 2ap + bp + a + b + c$$
$$= ap^2 + 2ap + bp + p$$

$an^2 + bn + c$ is therefore $(ap + 2a + b + 1)p$.

Find a similar expression for $an^2 + bn + c$ when $n = 1 + 2p$.

$an^2 + bn + c$ is divisible by p when $n = 1$, $n = 1 + p$ and $n = 1 + 2p$. If it is prime for each of these values then $an^2 + bn + c$ must equal p itself and we would have three points on a quadratic graph as shown.

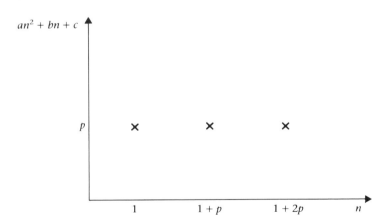

This is not possible for a quadratic.

So $an^2 + bn + c$ is **not** prime for at least one of these three values.

There may be some points on which you are still not convinced. If so, first try to fill in the necessary details yourself and then discuss the unclear points with fellow students and your teacher. Do not be convinced too easily!

Square and triangular grids

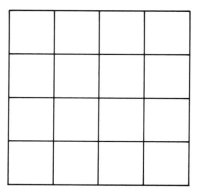

4 × 4 square grid

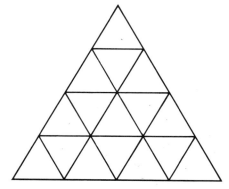

4 × 4 × 4 triangular grid

1 For the square grid find

    (a) the number of 1 × 1 squares,

    (b) the number of 2 × 2 squares,

    (c) the number of 3 × 3 squares,

    (d) the total number of squares in a 4 × 4 grid.

2 Find the total number of squares in a 5 × 5 grid.

3 Find the total number of triangles in a 4 × 4 × 4 triangular grid.

4 Find the total number of triangles in a 5 × 5 × 5 triangular grid.

Square and triangular grids

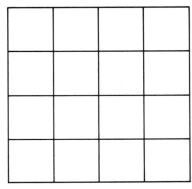

4 × 4 square grid

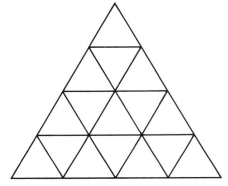

4 × 4 × 4 triangular grid

1   How many different sizes of square may be seen in the 4 × 4 square grid?

2   What is the total number of squares?

3   How many squares would there be in an $n \times n$ square grid?

4   Find the total number of triangles in the 4 × 4 × 4 triangular grid.

5   Find the total number of triangles in

(a) a 3 × 3 × 3 grid,

(b) a 5 × 5 × 5 grid.

6   Find a useful way of dividing the triangles in $n \times n \times n$ grids into two classes and hence conjecture the number of triangles in a 6 × 6 × 6 grid.

5 Mathematical articles

5.1 Introduction

The purpose of the chapter is to help you both **to read** and **to write** mathematics. It contains some pure and some 'real' case studies. These provide a model for writing mathematics and give an idea of what is expected when you write up your own investigations.

The first two case studies are interspersed with questions of the kind you should be asking yourself when you read a piece of mathematics. The questions should help you to develop your understanding and to check that the writer's argument is correct.

CASE STUDIES

1 – The Platonic solids (page 50)
2 – The gravity model in geography (page 54)

5.2 Reading mathematics

In reading the best mathematical writing a considerable effort of self-discipline is needed to keep going through to the end. (The same applies to the worst writing, but for different reasons!) In a good article, ideas will arise which suggest investigations not followed in the text and you may find it difficult to keep your mind on the job in hand. You can comfort yourself with the thought that side-lines can always be followed up later. Mathematical articles cannot be read as you would read a novel; the information content is usually very dense and you should take time to check calculations, verify assertions made and **understand thoroughly** the definitions and the argument as it develops.

Case studies 1 and 2 include questions interspersing the text at various stages. In the remaining case studies the exposition will be uninterrupted, all questions being set at the end. To help to bridge the gap between the two styles, here is an exercise based upon the beginning of an article published in *Mathematical Spectrum* (volume 19, number 1 (1986/87)).

E X E R C I S E   1

1   Read the following article carefully and carry out the necessary thinking and writing at all the points indicated by numbered asterisks.

2   The following questions are given at the end of the extract.

  (i) Can one draw a doodle without a 2-gon?

 (ii) Can one draw a doodle without a 3-gon?

(iii) Can one draw a doodle without either a 2-gon or a 3-gon?

Answers can be found in the original article, but you might like to try some doodles and see if you can answer 'yes' or 'no' yourself!

On doodles and 4-regular graphs

J.C. Turner, *University of Waikato*

Introduction

The next time you are doodling on a piece of paper, let your pen come back to its starting point and then consider what kind of mathematical figure you have drawn.

If you have always let your pen trace a smooth continuous curve, and whenever you have met a previous point on the curve you have crossed directly over the old curve, it is probable that you have drawn what graph-theorists call a 4-regular graph: figure 1 is an example.[*1] In this case n, the number of crossing points $= 9$, m, the number of edges (an edge is a curve joining two adjacent crossing points) $= 18$ and r, the number of regions (one is shown shaded, 34589) $= 11$, including the region of the plane exterior to the graph.[*2] Such diagrams are called *4-regular graphs* because every crossing point (these are usually called *vertices*, or *nodes*) has four edges adjoined to it.

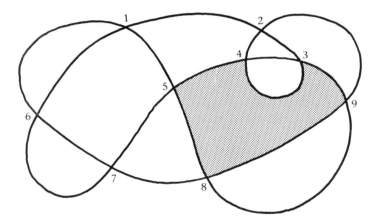

You might like to think what you would have to do whilst doodling if the result were not to be a 4-regular graph,[*3] and conversely, whether there are 4-regular graphs which are not doodles![*4] You might like to think of how many *small* regions (ones with few edges) you have managed to draw in your doodle.

Let us say a region is a *k-gon* if it is bounded by k edges. Then the smallest region possible is a 1-gon or loop; then a 2-gon; then a 3-gon; and so on. In the doodle shown in figure 1 there are four 2-gons and three 3-gons. There are also two 4-gons, one 5-gon, and the outer-region 6-gon.[*5]

The purpose of this article is to discuss the possibility of bounds on the frequencies of small regions in 4-regular graphs. Simple questions to ask are:

  (i) Can one draw a doodle without a 2-gon?

  (ii) Can one draw a doodle without a 3-gon?

  (iii) Can one draw a doodle without either a 2-gon or a 3-gon?

5.3 Case studies

> What reading strategy should you adopt when studying a piece of mathematical writing?

Whatever strategy you decide to adopt can be tested out and refined when tackling the remaining case studies. You should make a selection from these rather than attempt them all. We hope that you will find two or three which interest you.

CASE   STUDIES

After working through this chapter you should:

1   have developed a strategy for reading mathematical articles with understanding;

2   appreciate the need for a clear and orderly style when presenting a mathematical argument.

The Platonic solids

For $n = 3, 4, 5, \ldots$ there is precisely one shape of polygon with n equal sides and n equal angles. We say that there are infinitely many **regular polygons**.

> What do you understand by the term 'regular polygon'?
> What is meant by 'infinitely many' regular polygons?

A regular polygon is a two-dimensional shape. The analogous three-dimensional shape is a solid whose faces are congruent regular polygons with the same number of these polygons meeting at each vertex (or corner) of the solid.

Such solids were considered in Plato's *Timaeus* and became known as the Platonic solids.

> Name a three-dimensional shape which fits the description of a Platonic solid.

Given that there are infinitely many regular polygons, you might expect there to be infinitely many Platonic solids. We shall investigate whether or not this is the case.

To try to classify the Platonic solids systematically, we can start with solids with the 'simplest' possible faces: equilateral triangles.

CASE 1. EQUILATERAL TRIANGULAR FACES

To form a corner, at least three faces meet at any vertex. For triangular faces, at most five such faces meet at a vertex because if the angles at a vertex totalled 360° or more, then the faces could not form a corner.

> Explain fully why six triangular faces cannot meet at a vertex.

We need to consider the cases of three, four or five faces meeting at each vertex. As an example, let us examine the second possibility.

Four faces meet at each vertex.

It is easy to form the required solid by taping together equilateral triangles, four at each vertex. The shape obtained is known as the regular octahedron and has eight faces.

From a model of an octahedron we can verify the figures in the following table:

Number of faces,	F	8
Number of vertices,	V	6
Number of edges,	E	12

What are the values of F, V and E for a cube?

The mathematician Euler found that the equation $F + V = E + 2$ is true for all polyhedra.

Find $F + V - E$ for (a) the octahedron and (b) the cube.

Remarkably, we could have used Euler's formula to obtain the number of faces, vertices and edges of the octahedron without ever making the model!

We are looking for a shape formed by F triangular faces.

These have $3F$ sides and $3F$ corners. When they are taped together, each edge of the solid is formed from a pair of these sides and so

$$E = \frac{3F}{2}$$

Each vertex of the solid is formed from four corners and so

$$V = \frac{3F}{4}$$

Substituting these results into Euler's formula, we obtain

$$F + \frac{3F}{4} = \frac{3F}{2} + 2$$

$$\Rightarrow \quad 4F + 3F = 6F + 8$$

$$\Rightarrow \quad F = 8$$

Then $E = 12$ and $V = 6$, as required.

This kind of analysis can be very helpful in showing precisely what possibilities there are for particular solids. By a similar analysis, we can show that the only Platonic solids with three or five triangular faces at a vertex are the tetrahedron and the icosahedron.

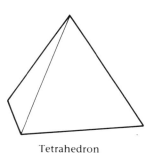

Tetrahedron

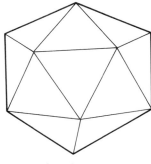

Icosahedron

Use Euler's formula to show that a Platonic solid with three triangular faces at each vertex must have precisely four faces.

CASE 2. SQUARE FACES

In this case three faces must meet at each vertex.

Explain the assertion above.

Substituting $E = \dfrac{4F}{2}$ and $V = \dfrac{4F}{3}$ into Euler's formula gives

$$F + \frac{4F}{3} = \frac{4F}{2} + 2$$

from which we obtain $F = 6$, $V = 8$ and $E = 12$. So the solid must be a cube.

Explain why $E = \dfrac{4F}{2}$ and $V = \dfrac{4F}{3}$.

CASE 3. FACES WITH FIVE OR MORE EDGES

Just three hexagons at a vertex give an angle of 360°. Therefore we need only consider the case of three regular pentagons meeting at each vertex because $4 \times 108°$ is greater than 360°.

> What is the significance of the 108° mentioned above?

A similar analysis to that carried out in cases 1 and 2 shows that a Platonic solid with pentagonal faces must have $F = 12$, $V = 20$, $E = 30$.

There is one such solid.

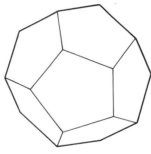

Dodecahedron

> Obtain the given values of F, V and E.

It is interesting that there should be infinitely many two-dimensional regular shapes yet only five regular three-dimensional shapes, the five Platonic solids: tetrahedron, octahedron, icosahedron, cube and dodecahedron. Mathematicians have shown that there are six regular four-dimensional 'solids' and, curiously, only three in any space of more than four dimensions – the n-dimensional cube, tetrahedron and octahedron.

The gravity model in geography

Newton's law of universal gravitation states that two bodies with masses m_1 and m_2 attract each other with a force

$$\frac{Gm_1m_2}{d^2}$$

where d is the distance between the centres of mass of the bodies and G is constant. This equation has been used successfully in modelling planetary motion, by Newton and others.

The term 'gravity model' is applied in geography in a looser way. Some authors use it of any model where the intensity of an interaction between places decreases with distance. The interaction could be one of trade or transportation or migration, for instance. Others insist upon a stricter analogy with Newton's model in which, if the two places had measures of attractiveness W_1 and W_2 and were separated by a distance d, then if T were some measure of the intensity of interaction between the places,

$$T = \frac{kW_1W_2}{d^\beta}$$

where k is a constant and β a positive number.

> What value does β have in Newton's model of gravitation?

TELEPHONE CALLS

Start with an example using a model closely resembling Newton's. The populations and distances separating towns are given below.

Town	Population (in thousands)	Distances (km) from	
		Sheffield	Derby
Sheffield	537	–	52
Derby	216	52	–
Nottingham	271	50	20

Suppose that the number of telephone calls made in a given time between town A and town B can be found using the equation

$$T_{AB} = \frac{kP_A P_B}{d_{AB}{}^2}$$

where k is a constant, P_A and P_B are the populations of towns A and B respectively and d_{AB} is the distance between them.

Using this model, the number of telephone calls between Sheffield and Derby is

$$T_{SD} = \frac{k \times 537 \times 216}{52^2} = 43k$$

If the model were to be used to predict numbers of calls between towns, it would first be tested with known data. This would enable the 'calibration' of the model, in which the value of k would be found. At the same time, a check would be made to find whether the inverse square model was most appropriate or whether some other exponent should be substituted for 2 in the formula for the number of telephone calls.

(a) Use the model to find T_{DN} and T_{SN}.

(b) Which pair of the towns of Sheffield, Derby and Nottingham has the most telephone calls between them according to the model?

TWO COMPETING SHOPPING CENTRES

If, in a rural area, there is a good network of roads and two towns satisfy the shopping needs of the scattered community, then the application of a simple gravity model may be considered.

Suppose towns A and B have populations P_A and P_B respectively. An individual lives at C which is distance d_A km from A and d_B km from B, as shown in the diagram.

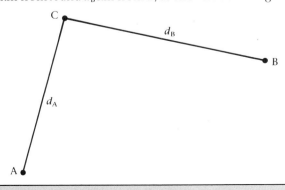

The gravity model suggests that the attractiveness of A to the individual is of the form

$$\frac{kP_A}{d_A{}^2}$$

> What is the attractiveness of B to the individual?

Now you can introduce the idea of an **area of influence**. If A is more attractive than B, then the individual is in A's area of influence, and vice versa.

First you should investigate this idea in a simple theoretical case. Suppose that A and B have populations of 40 000 and 10 000 respectively. Then for a point P, the attractiveness of

A is $\dfrac{40\,000\,k}{AP^2}$ and that of B is $\dfrac{10\,000\,k}{BP^2}$.

If A and B are equally attractive then

$$\frac{40\,000\,k}{AP^2} = \frac{10\,000\,k}{BP^2}$$

$$AP^2 = 4BP^2$$

$$AP = 2BP$$

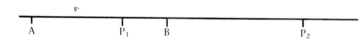

If P_1 divides AB in the ratio 2 : 1, then P_1 will be on the locus of points where A and B are equally attractive. Similarly, the point P_2 dividing AB externally in the ratio 2 : 1 will be on this locus.

If AB = $3a$ then it is not difficult to verify that

$$AP_2 = 6a, \qquad AP_1 = 2a, \qquad P_1P_2 = 4a$$

Now let AB be the x-axis and take as origin 0 the midpoint of P_1P_2.

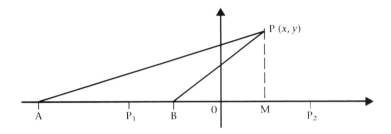

Let P (x, y) be any point on the locus of equal attractions. From the diagram

$$AP = 2BP$$
$$AP^2 = 4BP^2$$
$$AM^2 + PM^2 = 4(BM^2 + PM^2)$$
$$(x + AO)^2 + y^2 = 4(x + BO)^2 + 4y^2$$
$$(x + 4a)^2 + y^2 = 4(x + a)^2 + 4y^2$$
$$3x^2 + 3y^2 = 12a^2$$
$$x^2 + y^2 = 4a^2$$

This last equation will be recognised as that of the circle with P_1P_2 as diameter. All points inside the circle are in B's area of influence. Points outside the circle are in A's area of influence.

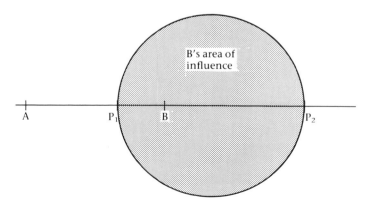

You can now apply the theory to an actual case.

The map shows the area around Wisbech and King's Lynn, whose populations are respectively 17 000 and 30 000. You may assume that they are the only shopping attractions in the area.

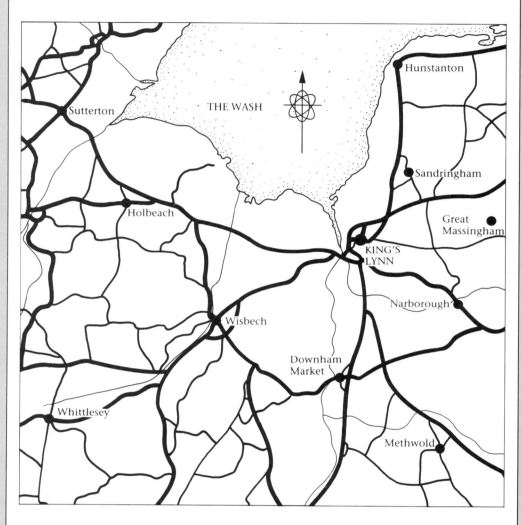

To find the areas of shopping influence of Wisbech and King's Lynn, consider someone for whom they are equally attractive, who lives distance d_W from Wisbech and distance d_L from King's Lynn.

$$\frac{k \times 17\,000}{d_W{}^2} = \frac{k \times 30\,000}{d_L{}^2}$$

So
$$17\,000\,d_L{}^2 = 30\,000\,d_W{}^2$$

You can take square roots to obtain $130d_L = 173d_W$.

People for whom this equation holds live on a circle whose centre lies somewhere along the line through Wisbech and King's Lynn. Two points on the circle's circumference, X and Y, are marked on the diagram below.

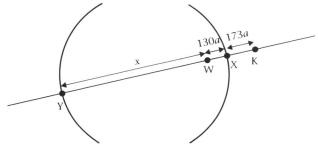

If the distance from Wisbech to King's Lynn is 13 miles, then in mile units $a = 0.043$ and the point X is 5.6 miles from Wisbech and 7.4 miles from King's Lynn.

> Explain the calculation that leads to $a = 0.043$.

To locate the point Y, find the distance x as follows:

$$\frac{x + 13}{x} = \frac{173}{130}$$

$$43x = 130 \times 13$$

$$x = 39.3$$

Therefore the point Y is 39.3 miles beyond Wisbech and the diameter of the circle is 44.9 miles.

> (a) Explain the statement
>
> $$\frac{x + 13}{x} = \frac{173}{130}$$
>
> (b) Shrewsbury and Welshpool are 19 miles apart and have populations of 56 000 and 7 000 respectively. Using the same gravity model, write down expressions for the attractiveness of the two towns to an individual who lives distance d_S from Shrewsbury and d_W from Welshpool.
>
> (c) Using the method outlined above, carry out the necessary calculations and describe as fully as possible Welshpool's area of influence.
>
> (d) In areas of the USA, it is easy to travel long distances by car. What difference would this make to the value of β taken in the model?

The game of Hex

The game of Hex was invented by Piet Hein in 1942 at Niels Bohr's Institute for Theoretical Physics in Copenhagen. A variation of this game, known as 'Blockbusters', is now a popular television quiz game.

The original game, for two players, is played on a diamond-shaped board made up of hexagons. One player has a set of white counters, the other a set of black counters. The players, White and Black, alternately place one of their counters on any vacant hexagon. The object of the game is for White to try to complete a chain of white counters between the two edges marked 'White', while Black tries to form a chain of black counters joining the 'Black' edges. The game ends as soon as one player completes such an unbroken chain.

Here is a diagram showing a game won by Black on a 4 × 4 board.

The game went as follows:

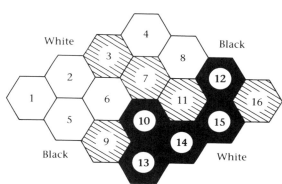

White	Black
3	10
7	15
11	14
16	12
9	13

Black wins because of the chain 13–14–15–12.

In this game, Black's first two moves, at 10 and 15, illustrate a useful tactic when playing Hex.

RESULT 1

Black cannot be prevented from connecting 10 and 15 because if White plays on 11 Black can play on 14, whereas if White plays on 14 Black can play on 11. Therefore, Black can always complete the chain 10–11/14–15.

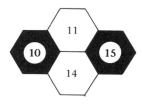

When playing the game, it is also helpful to know another type of connecting result.

RESULT 2

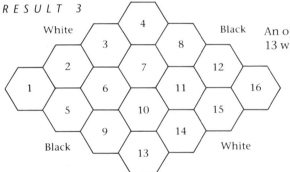

White

Black, to play, cannot prevent White connecting her counter on 1 to the White edge. For example, if Black plays on 2 or 4, White can simply play on 3 and then form the chain 1–3–6/7.

On small boards, the first player to move has such a strong advantage that she should always win. For example, White to play first on a 4 × 4 board will win easily, especially if she knows the following result, which is easy to prove with the help of result 2.

RESULT 3

White   Black

Black   White

An opening play by White on 4, 7, 10 or 13 wins. Any other opening play loses.

On larger boards it is much more difficult to make such a full analysis of the game and in practice an 11 × 11 board is used for serious games.

QUESTIONS

1 For result 2, show how White can connect 1 to the white edge when Black's initial move is 3, 6 or 7.

2 After the sample game of the article, White claimed that her third move, 11, was the losing one. She believed that she could have won the game by playing another move instead. Sketch the position immediately **before** her third move, and prove or disprove her claim.

3 For result 3, prove that White can force a win by playing at either 7 or 10.

Proportional representation

The British electoral system has often been criticised as being unfair, because the number of seats in Parliament won by any particular political party depends only on which particular party wins in each of the 650 constituencies. The votes cast for the other parties standing in the constituency do not affect the final make up of the parties at Westminster. Some people argue that the mix of MPs from the various parties should reflect the actual numbers of votes, using a system of proportional representation.

Proportional representation is based on the principle that the number of seats gained by a party should be directly proportional to the number of votes cast for the party.

One way of expressing the principle of proportional representation is

$$\frac{\text{Number of seats gained}}{\text{Total number of seats}} = \frac{\text{Number of votes gained}}{\text{Total number of votes}}$$

In the examples which follow, you should assume that the **total number of seats** refers to just one constituency and that each constituency will return several MPs and not just one as in the British system.

EXAMPLE 1

First, consider a fictitious constituency in which three parties stand for election. The constituency can return 6 MPs.

The votes cast during an election are

party A – 2000;   party B – 4000;   party C – 6000.

The result of the election in this constituency is

party A – 1 seat;   party B – 2 seats;   party C – 3 seats.

EXAMPLE 2

Example 1 is too simplistic because in reality the principle of proportional representation will nearly always result in fractional parts of seats, whereas only whole numbers of seats can actually be allocated. There is a problem in how to deal with these fractions fairly.

Suppose the fictitious constituency from example 1 can only return 5 MPs. Then, by direct use of the principle, the result of the election would be

party A – 0.83 seats;   party B – 1.67 seats;   party C – 2.50 seats.

One solution to this problem would be to allocate seats as follows:

party A – 1 seat;   party B – 2 seats;   party C – 2 seats;

but this seems unfair on party C.

CASE STUDY

4

EXAMPLE 3 THE D'HONDT RULE

One possible solution to the problem posed in example 2 is the system devised by the Belgian, Victor d'Hondt.

Suppose three parties stand for election in a constituency that can return 6 MPs. The votes cast during the election are:

  party A – 1700; party B – 4000; party C – 4300.

(i) Divide the number of votes cast for each party by 2, 3, 4, 5 . . . for as far as is necessary to produce the six highest numbers possible.

	Party A	Party B	Party C
	1700	4000	4300
divide by 2	850	2000	2150
divide by 3	567	1333	1433
divide by 4	425	1000	1075

(ii) There are to be 6 MPs, so write down the six highest numbers from the table in (i).

  C – 4300; B – 4000; C – 2150; B – 2000; A – 1700; C – 1433.

The smallest of these six numbers is called the **electoral quotient**, so here the electoral quotient is 1433.

(iii) The highest number for each party from (ii) is divided by the electoral quotient:

  C – 3.0; B – 2.8; A – 1.2.

(iv) These numbers are rounded down to give the election result:

  C – 3 seats; B – 2 seats; A – 1 seat.

QUESTIONS

1 What does example 1 illustrate? Describe in what way example 1 is unrealistic.

2 Why is the solution to the fractional seats problem, proposed in example 2, unfair on party C? Why cannot party C be awarded 3 seats?

3 In a certain constituency, four parties put up candidates for the 5 seats that are available. The votes cast for each party are: A – 17 920 (39.8%); B – 11 490 (25.6%); C – 11 170 (24.8%); D – 4420 (9.8%)

  (a) What are the election results according to the d'Hondt rule?

  (b) Have you any criticism of the d'Hondt rule in the light of these results? Which party appears to benefit from the d'Hondt rule?

Magic squares

16	3	2	13
5	10	11	8
9	6	7	12
4	15	14	1

This 'magic square' appears in a copper-print made in 1514 by the German artist Albrecht Dürer.

The number square has the 'magic' properties:

sum of rows = sum of columns = sum of diagonals,

each of the sums being the 'magic total' 34. Notice also that it uses the consecutive integers from 1 to 16 and that Dürer was able to incorporate the date 1514 in an appropriate place. In addition, the four corner numbers, the four 2×2 squares in the corners and the 2×2 square in the centre all have the magic total.

3	14	12	105
23	94	7	10
93	7	26	8
15	19	89	11

The more up-to-date square shown here has all the magic properties listed previously and you will see that the same five 2×2 squares as before have the magic total.

However, inevitably, the integers are not consecutive and there is the additional 'weakness' that the number 7 is repeated.

How many 4×4 magic squares are there? A little thought should convince you that they are infinite in number. Indeed, you can form as many as you like with the same magic total. The rest of this article investigates a way in which these squares may be made. Note first that the sum of any two 4×4 magic squares is also magic. For example:

16	3	2	13
5	10	11	8
9	6	7	12
4	15	14	1

+

3	14	12	105
23	94	7	10
93	7	26	8
15	19	89	11

=

19	17	14	118
28	104	18	18
102	13	33	20
19	34	103	12

You can check that the square on the right is magic.

Similarly, you can obtain a new magic square if you multiply all the entries in a given magic square by the same number. For instance, if you double all the numbers in Dürer's square you will obtain the square on the right.

32	6	4	26
10	20	22	16
18	12	14	24
8	30	28	2

The operations of multiplication and addition are both used in the general rule:

if $A, B, C, \ldots$ are magic squares of the same dimension and $\alpha, \beta, \gamma, \ldots$ are any numbers, then $M = \alpha A + \beta B + \gamma C + \ldots$ is magic.

It is interesting to search for a basic set of squares from which any magic square may be constructed using this general rule.

A likely candidate for such a basic set is that in which the entries in the square are all 0 or 1 and 1s occur just once in each row, column, diagonal and subsquare. There are eight such basic squares.

B_1
$$\begin{matrix} 1 & 0 & 0 & 0 \\ 0 & 0 & 1 & 0 \\ 0 & 0 & 0 & 1 \\ 0 & 1 & 0 & 0 \end{matrix}$$

B_2
$$\begin{matrix} 1 & 0 & 0 & 0 \\ 0 & 0 & 0 & 1 \\ 0 & 1 & 0 & 0 \\ 0 & 0 & 1 & 0 \end{matrix}$$

B_3
$$\begin{matrix} 0 & 0 & 0 & 1 \\ 1 & 0 & 0 & 0 \\ 0 & 0 & 1 & 0 \\ 0 & 1 & 0 & 0 \end{matrix}$$

B_4
$$\begin{matrix} 0 & 0 & 0 & 1 \\ 0 & 1 & 0 & 0 \\ 1 & 0 & 0 & 0 \\ 0 & 0 & 1 & 0 \end{matrix}$$

B_5
$$\begin{matrix} 0 & 0 & 1 & 0 \\ 1 & 0 & 0 & 0 \\ 0 & 1 & 0 & 0 \\ 0 & 0 & 0 & 1 \end{matrix}$$

B_6
$$\begin{matrix} 0 & 1 & 0 & 0 \\ 0 & 0 & 1 & 0 \\ 1 & 0 & 0 & 0 \\ 0 & 0 & 0 & 1 \end{matrix}$$

B_7
$$\begin{matrix} 0 & 0 & 1 & 0 \\ 0 & 1 & 0 & 0 \\ 0 & 0 & 0 & 1 \\ 1 & 0 & 0 & 0 \end{matrix}$$

B_8
$$\begin{matrix} 0 & 1 & 0 & 0 \\ 0 & 0 & 0 & 1 \\ 0 & 0 & 1 & 0 \\ 1 & 0 & 0 & 0 \end{matrix}$$

You will find that any 4×4 magic square can indeed be formed from this basic set using the general rule. For example Dürer's square is given by the combination:

$$9B_1 + 7B_2 + 6B_3 + 7B_4 - B_5 + 2B_6 + 3B_7 + B_8$$

The question then arises: is the set $S = \{B_1, B_2, \ldots, B_8\}$ irreducible, or can you form all 4×4 magic squares from some subsets of S? In fact, as you can check,

$$B_1 + B_4 + B_5 + B_8 = B_2 + B_3 + B_6 + B_7$$

so that any member of the set S can be expressed in terms of the other seven. For example:

$$B_8 = B_2 + B_3 + B_6 + B_7 - B_1 - B_4 - B_5$$

This, in turn, means that according to the general rule any combination of the eight basic squares may be replaced by a combination of any seven. For example, the Dürer square can be expressed as

$$8B_1 + 8B_2 + 7B_3 + 6B_4 - 2B_5 + 3B_6 + 4B_7$$

It may be shown that you cannot reduce the basic set any further, so

$$G = \{B_1, B_2, B_3, B_4, B_5, B_6, B_7\}$$

is an irreducible generating set for 4×4 magic squares.

QUESTIONS

1 Why is the 'more up-to-date' square so called? What is its magic total? Why is it inevitable that the integers should not be consecutive?

2 Write down the magic square given by

$$B_1 - 2B_2 + 3B_3 - 4B_4 + 5B_5 - 6B_6 + 7B_7$$

3 Express the square

3	6	12	7
8	11	7	2
10	7	3	8
7	4	6	11

as a combination formed from the set G, using the general rule.

4 Form a magic square with magic total 100 and the year of your birth in the positions where Dürer had 1514.

5 Show that the relation

$$B_7 = aB_1 + bB_2 + cB_3 + dB_4 + eB_5 + fB_6$$

where a, b, c, d, e and f are whole numbers, is impossible.

Explain why the set G is irreducible.

6 Can the Dürer square be expressed in terms of members of the set G in a way different from that given in the article? If so, how? If not, why not?

Can you draw any more general conclusion?

Communications satellites

Satellites placed in geostationary orbit at various positions in space provide an important link in our method of rapid communication between two cities on the earth's surface. Although we tend to use the word 'stationary' to describe these satellites, they are in fact moving in circular paths with the centre of the earth as centre of each path. However, a satellite does remain above a particular point on the earth's surface so that it can be considered as 'fixed' relative to that point and so to an observer on earth the satellite appears to be stationary.

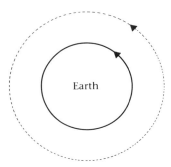

Communication signals are sent from the earth to a satellite and back to a receiving station. To go further round the earth, the signal is transmitted again to a second satellite and sent back. In this way, a city C can receive messages from city A, although city C is 'round the back' of the earth relative to A.

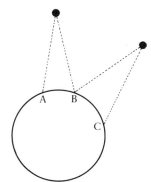

Various problems arise in connection with satellites in stationary orbit. For an organisation such as NASA or the European Space Agency, there is the problem of knowing the relation between the speed of the satellite and the height above the earth which gives a stationary orbit, that is one having a period of 24 hours.

For the telecommunications world, the problem is to find the number of satellites required so that any two points on the earth's surface can communicate with one another.

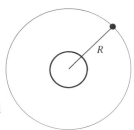

To simplify the physical situation, consider a system of communications satellites to provide links between points on the equator.

Suppose that a satellite has mass m kg and moves with constant speed v m s^{-1} in a circular orbit of radius R m.

For a geostationary orbit, the period, or the time for one complete revolution, is 24 hours. In terms of R and v, the period T in seconds is

$$T = \frac{2\pi R}{v} = 24 \times 60 \times 60$$

so that $\quad R = \left(\dfrac{12 \times 60 \times 60}{\pi}\right) v \qquad (1)$

The force in newtons acting on the satellite is given by Newton's law of gravitation as

$$\frac{GMm}{R^2}$$

where G is the constant of gravitation and M the mass of the earth in kg. Using Newton's second law,

$$m\frac{v^2}{R} = \frac{GMm}{R^2}$$

giving a second relation between v and R,

$\quad Rv^2 = GM \qquad (2)$

where $G = 6.67 \times 10^{-11}$ and $M = 5.98 \times 10^{24}$.

From equations (1) and (2),

$$\frac{12 \times 60 \times 60}{\pi} v^3 = GM$$

$$\Rightarrow \quad v^3 = \frac{\pi}{12 \times 60 \times 60} \times 6.67 \times 10^{-11} \times 5.98 \times 10^{24}$$

$$\Rightarrow \quad v \approx 3.07 \times 10^3$$

Then $\quad R = \dfrac{12 \times 60 \times 60}{\pi} v$

$$\Rightarrow \quad R \approx 4.22 \times 10^7$$

A geostationary satellite must have a velocity of 3.07×10^3 m s^{-1}. The radius of the earth is 6.4×10^6 m and so the satellite's height is approximately 3.6×10^4 kilometres.

CASE STUDY

QUESTIONS

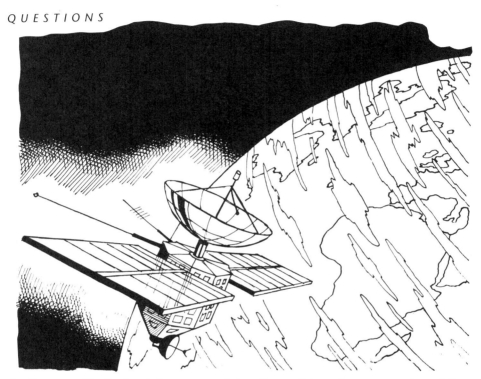

1 Can a satellite be fixed above any point on the earth's surface or are only certain points possible?

2 Why must the period of a geostationary satellite's orbit be 24 hours?

3 Explain why $\quad T = \dfrac{2\pi R}{v}$

and why $T = 24 \times 60 \times 60$.

4 Explain how the earth's radius was used to derive the height of 3.6×10^4 kilometres.

5 For any body moving in a circle there is an acceleration towards the centre of the circle. By looking at the equation derived from Newton's second law, above, determine an expression for this acceleration.

6 Consider a planet with radius 3000 km, mass 8×10^{23} kg and period of revolution 20 hours. Calculate the velocity and height above the planet's surface for a geostationary satellite tracing a path above a point on this planet's equator.

Queues on the M5

One of the aims of motorway design is to allow motorists to travel quickly and safely to their destinations avoiding the many villages and towns on their routes. This aim can usually be achieved on open stretches of the road. But all too often three-lane motorways are reduced to two lanes or two-lane motorways reduced to one lane because of surface repairs, central barrier repairs and so on. A trouble-free journey on a British motorway is almost a luxury and a motorist needs to allow extra journey time for long queues.

Suppose that a two-lane motorway is reduced to one lane for road repairs. At what safe speed should the traffic travel to allow the maximum possible number of vehicles through the section? To proceed with this problem you first need to make some simplifying assumptions.

Assume that all vehicles are cars of the same length, L metres, travelling with speed V m.p.h. with a distance of D metres between the fronts of any two cars.

Suppose that in the single carriageway section of the motorway the number of cars passing an observer each minute is N. N must be as large as possible, but because it is related to V and D there will be restrictions on its value. You therefore need the formula that relates N, V and D.

You must be careful with the mix of units. First convert V m.p.h. to metres per second.

$$V \text{ m.p.h.} = \frac{V}{60 \times 60} \text{ miles per second}$$

$$= \frac{V}{3600} \times \frac{8}{5} \text{ km per second}$$

$$= \frac{8V}{18\,000} \times 1000 \text{ metres per second}$$

$$= \frac{4}{9} V \text{ metres per second}$$

The car covers the distance D in

$$\frac{D}{\frac{4}{9}V} = \frac{9D}{4V} \text{ seconds.}$$

Therefore N cars pass the observer in $\dfrac{9ND}{4V}$ seconds and so

$$\frac{9ND}{4V} = 60 \quad \Rightarrow \quad N = \frac{80V}{3D}$$

When observing traffic on motorways, you should notice that the distance between vehicles becomes greater as their speeds increase. For example, on a three-lane motorway cars are often closer together in the slower inside lane than in the middle lane where they travel more quickly. The Highway Code recommends that vehicles should travel at a 'safe stopping distance' from the vehicle in front. This consists of two distances, a 'thinking distance' and a 'braking distance'. The following table shows these recommended distances at various speeds.

Speed (m.p.h.)	Thinking distance (metres)	Braking distance (metres)	Overall stopping distance (metres)
30	10	15	25
50	17	42	59
70	23	82	105

The overall stopping distance in metres is given by the formula

$$\frac{V}{3} + \frac{V^2}{60}$$

and so $D = L + \dfrac{V}{3} + \dfrac{V^2}{60}.$

You now have a model for the number of cars per minute passing an observation point, expressed by the equation

$$N = \frac{80}{3} \frac{V}{\left(L + \dfrac{V}{3} + \dfrac{V^2}{60}\right)}$$

Assuming a typical car length is about 4 m, this equation leads to the following table.

Speed V (m.p.h.)	5	10	15	20	25	30	35
N (cars per minute)	21	29	31	30	29	27	25

QUESTIONS

1   Explain why it is necessary to make the simplifying assumptions regarding L, V and D for **all** cars.

2   What is the approximate number of metres in 1 mile, as used in the calculations above?

3   Explain why $\dfrac{9ND}{4V} = 60$ and explain carefully how the equation $N = \dfrac{80V}{3D}$ is then derived.

4   Verify that

$$\frac{V}{3} + \frac{V^2}{60}$$

is a good approximation for the overall stopping distances as given in the table.

5   Explain why L must be added to the overall stopping distance to obtain the formula for D.

6   (a) What speed does the table suggest gives the maximum value of N?

   (b) How many car lengths apart are the cars at this speed?

Stock control

Have you ever been shopping for a particular item and found that the shop did not have it in stock? There are many reasons why shops do not always have a full stock of goods.

An unexpected increase in demand can deplete the stock. The amount of stock that a shop carries will clearly depend upon available storage space and this may be very limited. Carrying a large volume of stock ties up capital which could be earning interest if invested, so the shop will not want to carry more stock than is necessary.

The problem is to decide the best policy for stock control. The stock control model must determine how much stock is bought and when such a purchase takes place. You can develop a model for stock control which depends upon several factors.

The factors considered in this model are demand, interest rate, ordering cost and value of the items in stock. The aim of the policy is to minimise the cost of operation.

The model is developed in four stages, by considering:

(a) demand for the goods,

(b) the value of goods kept in stock,

(c) the cost of the stock control policy,

(d) minimising the cost.

(a)   D E M A N D   F O R   T H E   G O O D S

Many shops will learn from experience what demand there is for various goods and how this demand varies from month to month. **Assume** that demand is constant; there are no seasonal or other fluctuations. It must be stressed that this is an assumption and the results derived from this model depend crucially on this assumption. With the assumption of constant demand, it is possible to draw a graph of stock level against time.

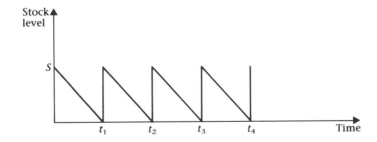

A few words of explanation may help to clarify how the graph illustrates the time variation of the stock level. The shop begins ($t = 0$) with an initial stock level of S. Since the demand is constant this level will be depleted steadily, resulting in the straight line meeting the time axis at t_1. At t_1 the stock level is 0 and so stock is reordered and the level then rises back to S. This cycle is repeated. At this stage, S, t_1, t_2, . . . are unknown.

Let n be the number of orders placed in a year and D the quantity ordered each year.

Then $nS = D \Rightarrow n = \dfrac{D}{S}$.

Since n orders are placed in 1 year, the time between orders is $\dfrac{1}{n}$ years.

(b) VALUE OF GOODS KEPT IN STOCK

Suppose the value of a single item is £V. For the previous saw-tooth graph,

maximum number of items in stock = S
minimum number of items in stock = 0

The stock varies linearly from S to 0 and so the average level is $\frac{1}{2}S$ stock is £$\frac{1}{2}SV$.

(c) COST OF STOCK CONTROL POLICY

There are two costs incurred in this stock control policy: the cost of placing the orders and the loss of interest on money tied up in stock.

(i) Order cost

Administrative costs are incurred each time an order is placed. Suppose each order costs £p to place and administer. n orders are placed per year. Then ordering costs per year are

$$\pounds np = \pounds\frac{Dp}{S}$$

(ii) Loss of interest

Money tied up in stock could be invested and earning interest so the loss of interest is a cost of the stock control policy. If the interest rate is r % p.a. and the average value of the stock is £ $\frac{1}{2}SV$, then the interest lost in 1 year is £ $\frac{1}{2}SV \times \frac{1}{100} r$.

Taking the two costs together, the total operating cost of the policy is £C, where

$$C = \frac{Dp}{S} + \frac{SVr}{200}$$

CASE STUDY

8

(d) MINIMISING THE COST

Most shops would choose to minimise costs, though sometimes other criteria are used in planning a stock control strategy.

In the expression for total cost, all parameters other than S are fixed. The value of S which minimises total cost is $\sqrt{\dfrac{200Dp}{Vr}}$. This value of S is called the **economic order quantity (EOQ)**.

QUESTIONS

1 How is n related to $t_1, t_2, t_3, \ldots$?

2 What is the number of items sold each year (the **demand**) in the model of stock control?

3 What does it mean to say that the 'stock varies linearly from S to 0'?

4 What criteria other than minimising costs might be used for a stock control policy?

5 In a year, an electrical firm sells 300 washing machines costing £200 each. Administrative costs per order are £35 and the annual interest rate is 12%.

  (a) What is the economic order quantity?

  (b) How often should orders be placed?

  (c) What is the annual cost of pursuing this policy?

  (d) If the price of a washing machine increases by 20%, what is the percentage change in the order quantity?

6 For this question, answer **either** (a) **or** (b).

  (a) Obtain the formula given for the EOQ using calculus.

  (b) Verify your answer to 5(a) using a graphical method.

7 A firm sells 26 items per month. The ordering cost is £1.50 per order and the current interest rate is 18%. The cost of the item depends upon the order size, x.

$$V = \begin{cases} 24 & \text{if } x < 20 \\ 20 & \text{if } 20 \le x < 50 \\ 16 & \text{if } x \ge 50 \end{cases}$$

Draw a graph of total operating costs against order size (take n from 0 to 70).

What is the EOQ?

Pecking orders

Whenever two hens in a barnyard compete for the same grain of food, the dominant hen gets its own way by pecking the other hen. The weaker hen does not peck back but simply searches for other food. Biologists study closely such pecking behaviour for the insights it gives into social relationships. The problem is to investigate how many possible 'pecking orders' there are for a barnyard with n hens.

The problem is only of interest for $n \geq 3$.

For simplicity, start by looking at the case $n = 3$. If the 3 hens are called A, B and C, then the eight 'network diagrams' below show all the possible pecking orders ($\rightarrow$ stands for 'pecks').

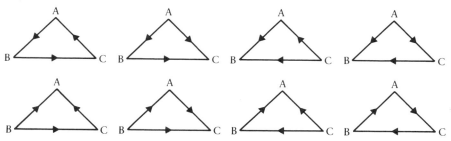

The diagrams show that there are eight pecking orders altogether.

The diagrams for $n = 3$ are of just two types,

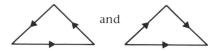

and

The behaviour represented by the first diagram is not observed in practice. Pecking is what is called a **transitive** relationship, i.e. if A pecks B and B pecks C, then A pecks C. Such a transitive relationship orders the hens into a chain

$$A \rightarrow B \rightarrow C$$

in the same way as the relationship '>' or 'is greater than' orders a set of real numbers.

For $n = 3$, there are just 3 ways of choosing the dominant hen and 2 ways of choosing the next hen in the hierarchy, giving $3 \times 2 \times 1$ or $3!$ possible transitive pecking orders. In general, for n hens, there are $n!$ transitive pecking orders.

Although this solves the barnyard problem, there is still the mathematical problem of the number of possible networks if you do not insist that the relationship must be transitive.

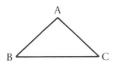

For $n = 3$, a neat way of obtaining the number 8 of possible networks is to observe that each of the 3 lines joining A, B and C can have an arrow in one of two directions and there are therefore $2 \times 2 \times 2 = 2^3$ possibilities.

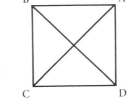

For 4 points there are 6 possible lines and therefore 2^6 possibilities.

For n points, each point is joined to $n-1$ others and so the product $n(n-1)$ counts each line twice.

Therefore there are $\frac{1}{2}n(n-1)$ lines and $2^{n(n-1)/2}$ possibilities.

An interesting (but difficult!) mathematical problem concerns how many 'types' of possible network there are for n points. For $n = 3$ you saw that there were 2. For $n = 4$ there are precisely 4. Two of these are given below, together with their associated **dominance sets**. Each point is labelled according to the number of other points it 'dominates' and these numbers are then put in decreasing numerical order.

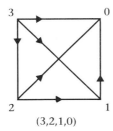

(3,2,1,0)

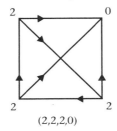

(2,2,2,0)

QUESTIONS

1 Why do you think the author claimed that the problem was 'only of interest for $n \geq 3$'?

2 What form of notation is used to represent the relationship 'A pecks B'?

3 Carefully explain the way in which the networks

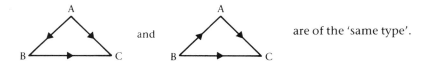

are of the 'same type'.

4 Is the network shown 'transitive'? Fully explain your answer.

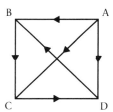

5 Explain why 'the product $n(n-1)$ counts each line twice'. Use the case $n = 4$ to illustrate your answer.

6 What are the two dominance sets for the case $n = 3$?

7 For $n = 4$, draw network diagrams corresponding to the dominance sets $(3, 1, 1, 1)$ and $(2, 2, 1, 1)$.

8 Explain

(a) why the numbers in a dominance set always total $\frac{1}{2}n(n-1)$,

(b) how you can recognise a dominance set corresponding to a transitive network.

10

Archimedes and π

π may be defined as the ratio of the circumference of a circle to its diameter:

$$\pi = \frac{\text{circumference}}{\text{diameter}}$$

The aim is to estimate the value of π by finding sequences of converging upper and lower bounds for the circumference of a circle of radius 1 unit. This method was used by the Greek mathematician Archimedes.

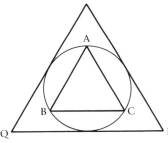

In the diagram,

$$\begin{array}{ccc} \text{perimeter of} & < & \text{circumference} & < & \text{perimeter of} \\ \text{triangle ABC} & & \text{of the circle} & & \text{triangle PQR} \end{array}$$

The two triangles are equilateral. The circle has radius 1 unit, so its circumference is 2π units. Let O be the centre of the circle.

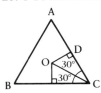

As AC is a chord of the circle, the line OD bisects it at right angles and so

$$DC = \cos 30° = \frac{\sqrt{3}}{2}$$

The perimeter of the triangle ABC is then $3\sqrt{3}$.

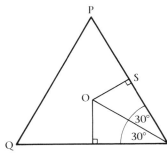

For triangle PQR, the sides PQ, QR and PR form tangents to the circle and so, for example, line OS bisects PR at right angles.

Then $SR = \cot 30° = \sqrt{3}$ and the perimeter of triangle PQR is $6\sqrt{3}$.

So the first upper and lower bounds for π are given by $\dfrac{3\sqrt{3}}{2} < \pi < 3\sqrt{3}$

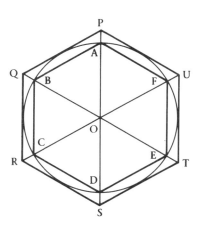

The figure shows a regular hexagon ABCDEF, **inscribed** within the circle, and a regular hexagon PQRSTU, **circumscribed** around the circle.

You require the lengths of the perimeters of both these hexagons.

Since the circle has radius 1, you know that both OM and AB are 1 unit long, so the perimeter of the *inscribed* hexagon is 6.

The circumscribed hexagon is an enlargement of the inscribed hexagon by scale factor $\dfrac{OM}{OL}$. By Pythagoras'

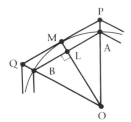

theorem, $OL = \sqrt{1 - \left(\dfrac{1}{2}\right)^2} = \dfrac{\sqrt{3}}{2}$ and so the scale factor of the enlargement is $\dfrac{2}{\sqrt{3}}$.

It follows that the perimeter of the circumscribed hexagon is $\dfrac{12}{\sqrt{3}}$ or $4\sqrt{3}$, and so

$3 < \pi < 2\sqrt{3}$.

To bring the upper and lower bounds for π still closer together you need to consider polygons with more than 6 sides.

A polygon with n sides is called an 'n-gon'. You can demonstrate that it is possible to calculate the length of the side of a regular $2n$-gon inscribed in the circle from the length of the side of the regular inscribed n-gon.

You can use an enlargement argument, similar to that for the hexagon case above, to find the perimeters of the circumscribing n-gon and $2n$-gon, so you can extend your sequences of converging upper and lower bounds for π.

Let x_n be the length of the side of a regular inscribed n-gon,
I_n be the perimeter of a regular inscribed n-gon, $I_n = nx_n$,
C_n be the perimeter of a regular circumscribed n-gon.

An enlargement argument, similar to that used in the hexagon case, gives

$$C_n = \frac{I_n}{\sqrt{1 - \dfrac{x_n^2}{4}}}$$

You can obtain a regular inscribed 2n-gon from the regular inscribed n-gon by drawing the line of symmetry of each triangle OAB, OBC etc., to obtain triangles OAM, OMB, OBN, ONC, etc., as shown in the diagram.

Now

$$AM^2 = AL^2 + LM^2 \quad \text{(Pythagoras' theorem)}$$

$$= \left(\frac{x_n}{2}\right)^2 + (1 - OL)^2$$

But $OL^2 = OA^2 - AL^2 = 1 - \left(\dfrac{x_n}{2}\right)^2$

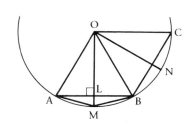

So $AM^2 = \left(\dfrac{x_n}{2}\right)^2 + \left[1 - \sqrt{1 - \left(\dfrac{x_n}{2}\right)^2}\,\right]^2$

That is $x_{2n} = \sqrt{\dfrac{x_n^2}{4} + \left[1 - \sqrt{1 - \dfrac{x_n^2}{4}}\,\right]^2}$

These equations make it possible to find successive approximations for π as shown in the table.

n	x_n	I_n	C_n	Inequality
3	$\sqrt{3}$	$3\sqrt{3}$	$6\sqrt{3}$	$\dfrac{3\sqrt{3}}{2} < \pi < 3\sqrt{3}$
6	1	6	$4\sqrt{3}$	$3 < \pi < 2\sqrt{3}$
12				
24				

You may like to continue the table and so find π to any desired accuracy.

QUESTIONS

1   Explain what is meant by 'converging upper and lower bounds'.

2   Give a detailed explanation of why

(a) $DC = \cos 30°$;   (b) $SR = \cot 30°$.

3   Show how the two results from question 2 lead to the inequality

$$\frac{3\sqrt{3}}{2} < \pi < 3\sqrt{3}$$

4   Explain the meaning of the terms: (a) inscribed;   (b) circumscribed.

5   Justify the statement 'you know both OM and AB are 1 unit long, so the perimeter of the inscribed hexagon is 6'.

6   (a) Give the details of the calculations leading to the value of $4\sqrt{3}$ for the perimeter of the circumscribed hexagon.

(b) Show how this results in the inequality $3 < \pi < 2\sqrt{3}$.

7   Give the details of the argument that

$$C_n = \frac{I_n}{\sqrt{1 - \dfrac{x_n^2}{4}}}$$

8   (a) Write down the formula for x_{12} in terms of x_6.

(b) Hence find x_{12}.

9   Showing all details of the working, complete the row of the table for $n = 12$.

10   Explain how continuing the table would lead to a value of π of any desired accuracy.

6 Starting points

6.1 Using this chapter

We hope that other parts of your mathematics course will provide interesting starting points for some mathematical work of your own. Alternatively, another school subject or a hobby or interest pursued outside school may suggest ideas. You are free to explore problems which interest you personally!

The various problems contained in this chapter are therefore provided only as suggestions. Usually no approach to the solution is included in the text and you should discuss the problem with your teacher if you find it difficult to make headway.

The problems are intended to be 'open' in the sense that there are no 'model answers'. You are free to investigate and develop those aspects of the problems which interest you. When appropriate, you should try to demonstrate in your work the processes which have been discussed earlier in this unit:

- looking at particular cases;
- forming patterns;
- generalisation;
- proof;
- model formulation;
- interpretation/validation;

  and so on.

6.2 'Pure' problems

1 BILLARDS

Imagine a billiard table with dimensions x and y units, where x and y are whole numbers. There are 'pockets' at each corner. The ball begins either at a corner or at an integer distance from a corner. It moves at an angle of 45° to the side, and rebounds from a cushion at an angle of 90° to its previous direction of motion.

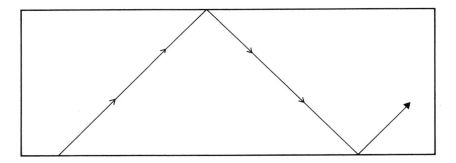

Investigate the possible paths of a ball.

2 CHAINS – DIVISORS

The numbers which divide 12, and are smaller than 12, are 1, 2, 3, 4 and 6. Add these divisors: $1 + 2 + 3 + 4 + 6 = 16$. Write $12 \rightarrow 16$.

Repeat the procedure for 16. Its divisors are 1, 2, 4, 8.
Add: $1 + 2 + 4 + 8 = 15$. Write $12 \rightarrow 16 \rightarrow 15$.

Repeat the procedure until you have

$$12 \rightarrow 16 \rightarrow 15 \rightarrow 9 \rightarrow 4 \rightarrow 3 \rightarrow 1$$

Investigate with other numbers.

(a) Some numbers go to bigger numbers: for example $12 \rightarrow 16$. These are called **abundant** numbers. Can you find more abundant numbers, and a pattern within them?

(b) Numbers which go to smaller numbers are called **deficient** numbers (for example $9 \rightarrow 4$). Investigate these.

(c) Note that $6 \curvearrowright 6$ and $28 \curvearrowright 28$. These are called **perfect** numbers. Investigate.

(d) $220 \curvearrowright 284$. Can you find smaller pairs? (Pairs such as 220 and 284 are called **friendly** numbers.)

3 TRIANGLE – SQUARE NUMBERS

The triangular numbers are 1, 3, 6, 10, . . ., $\frac{1}{2}n(n+1)$, . . .

The square numbers are 1, 4, 9, 16, . . ., m^2, . . .

Which numbers are both triangular and square? The first two are 1 and 36.

4 CHAINS – REORDERING DIGITS

Any four-digit number is rewritten with its digits arranged in ascending and descending order of size. The smaller is then subtracted from the larger and the process is repeated.

Example: 7345 gives $7543 - 3457 = 4086$
         4086 gives $8640 - 0468 = 8172$
         Then write $7543 \rightarrow 8640 \rightarrow 8721 \rightarrow \ldots$

Complete this chain and then try again with other four-digit numbers.

Now try with 3 or 5 or 6 or n digits.

5 STAMPS

A small mail-order firm finds that it is constantly running out of stamps of the right denomination, so it calls on Professor Schomp for help. 'Buy lots of 3p and 5p stamps' is his advice.

Examine this reply and consider related situations.

6 SOLUTION IN INTEGERS

In the equation

$$x^2 - y^2 = m^n$$

x, y, m and n are all integers. Investigate the possibility of solutions in the cases

(a) $m = 1$ (b) $m > 1, n > 2$ (c) $m > 1, n = 2$

7 CYCLIC ARRANGEMENTS OF DIGITS

Take any three-digit multiple of 37,
for example $7 \times 37 = 259$.
Arrange the digits of 259 in a cycle:

and construct the other two numbers having the same three digits in the same cyclic order, 592 and 925.

Both these are also multiples of 37:

$592 = 16 \times 37$ and $925 = 25 \times 37$.

Explain why this happens and construct similar examples.

8 RECURRING DECIMALS

$\frac{1}{7} = 0.\dot{1}4285\dot{7}$

$\frac{2}{7} = 0.\dot{2}8571\dot{4}$

$\frac{3}{7} = 0.\dot{4}2857\dot{1}$

Starting with some observations on these and other particular cases, write an account of recurring decimals.

9 INTEGRAL PART

For positive integers n, let

$$p(n) = [n + \sqrt{n} + \tfrac{1}{2}]$$

where the square brackets represent the integral part (written INT in computer language).

Which values does $p(n)$ not take, and why?

10 DIVISORS OF N

12 can be written as the product of two positive divisors (factors) in six different ways:

$$12 = 1 \times 12 = 2 \times 6 = 3 \times 4 = 4 \times 3 = 6 \times 2 = 12 \times 1$$

You can look at it in a slightly different way and say that 12 has six divisors, 1, 2, 3, 4, 6 and 12.

Define $d(N)$ to be the number of positive integers dividing N. So

$$d(12) = 6$$

What can you say about $d(N)$ for different integers N? Prove any statements you make.

1 1 AVERAGE NUMBER OF DIVISORS

Let $d(N)$ be the number of divisors of N, defined above. Now define $D(N)$, the average number of divisors for numbers up to N, by

$$D(N) = \frac{1}{N} \sum_{n=1}^{N} d(n)$$

By relating $D(N)$ to the number of lattice points on or under the graph of $y = \dfrac{N}{x}$, find the limit of $D(N)$ for large N. (A lattice point is a point with integer coordinates.)

1 2 RAILWAY LAYOUTS

A railway set contains a large number of pieces of rail, each in the form of a quadrant of a circle.

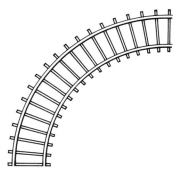

These can be joined together to make **layouts**:

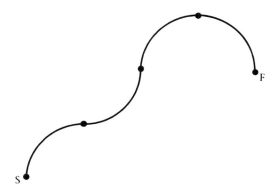

and the layouts can be described by 'words' consisting of R for right and L for left. If the layout above starts at S and finishes at F its word is R L R R.

Some layouts are closed.

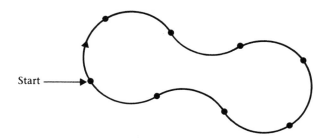

Start

These are called **circuits**. The diagram above shows the circuit
R R L R R R L R.

Given a word consisting of a large number of Rs and Ls, how would
you tell (without drawing the layout) whether or not it represented a
circuit?

13 WRONG DELIVERIES

A postman has 4 letters to deliver, one for each of 4 flats. In how
many ways can he deliver them so that each is in a wrong box (and
no two go into the same box)?

Try the same problem for 5 letters for 5 flats and explore the
possibility of obtaining a general result.

14 TOWERS OF HANOI

Suppose you have a stand with three vertical pegs, on the first of
which is a tower of n circular discs of decreasing radii, as shown in
the diagram below. The problem is to find the smallest number of
moves needed to transfer the tower onto the second peg, by moving
just one disc at a time onto another peg, and subject to the
condition that at no stage may any disc be placed above a smaller
disc.

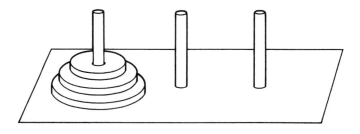

15 GARDEN PATH

A garden path is to be laid with rectangular slabs, each of width 1 unit and length 2 units. If the length of the path is *n* units, in how many ways can this be done? (Consider various widths of path.)

16 CUBIC GRAPHS

What 'different' graphs are possible for the cubic function

$$y = a + bx + cx^2 + dx^3 ?$$

Explain how the shape is related to the values of the coefficients *a, b, c, d*.

Investigate possible shapes of graphs of polynomial functions of degree more than 3.

17 PEBBLES

Fifteen pebbles are placed on the table; two players, in turn, take one, two or three pebbles until all pebbles are taken. The player who then holds an odd number of pebbles wins. Investigate winning strategies and extend the problem.

18 TESSELLATING POLYGONS

Make a list of the interior angles of regular polygons. Determine which groupings of regular polygons can be arranged to fit edge to edge in contact around a shared vertex so that there are no gaps:

(a) when the regular polygons must all be identical;

(b) when two or more different polygons are allowed.

Use these results to investigate what tessellations of the plane are possible using only regular polygons.

19 BUILDING A 'BRIDGE'

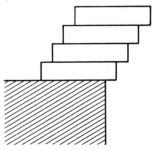

A 'bridge' is to be built to extend as far as possible over a chasm, but it is to be built with bricks and without mortar, supported by the edge of the chasm, and from one side only (see the diagram). How far can the 'bridge' be extended beyond the edge of the chasm?

89

20 INTEGRAL TRIANGLES

How many different triangles having sides of integer lengths can be drawn having a longest side (or sides) of length n units?

21 SUMS OF DIAGONALS

Investigate the sums of the diagonals of slopes 1, 2, 3, 4, . . . in the infinite grid below.

Two diagonals of slopes 1 and 2 are illustrated.

1	2	3	4	5	6	7	8	9	10	·	·
2	4	6	8	10	12	14	16	18	20	·	·
3	6	9	12	15	18	21	24	27	30	·	·
4	8	12	16	20	24	28	32	36	40	·	·
5	10	15	20	25	30	35	40	45	50	·	·
6	12	18	24	30	36	42	48	54	60	·	·
7	14	21	28	35	42	49	56	63	70	·	·
8	16	24	32	40	48	56	64	72	80	·	·
9	18	27	36	45	54	63	72	81	90	·	·
10	20	30	40	50	60	70	80	90	100	·	·
·	·	·	·	·	·	·	·	·	·		
·	·	·	·	·	·	·	·	·	·		

22 NO TRIANGLES

Points are marked on the circumference of a circle and lines are drawn joining pairs of these points. What is the largest possible number of lines if no three of the points are allowed to form the vertices of a triangle?

6.3 'Real' problems

1 PROPORTIONAL REPRESENTATION

Look at the table below. It gives data for British general elections from 1918 to 1970.

	Conservative		Liberal		Labour		Others	
	% votes	% seats	% votes	% seats	% votes	% seats	% votes	% seats
1918	35	54	23	23.5	5	10	27	12.5
1922	39	56	29	18.5	28.5	23	2.5	2.5
1923	38	42	29.5	26	30.5	31	2	1
1924	47	67	18	6.5	33	24.5	2	2
1929	38	42	23.5	10	37	47	1.5	1
1931	55	76	11	12	30	8.5	4	3.5
1935	54	70	6.5	3	37.5	25	2	2
1945	40	33	9	2	48	62	3	3
1950	43	47.8	9	1.5	46	50.4	2	0.3
1951	48	50.5	2.5	1	48.5	47	1	0.5
1955	49.8	55	2.7	0.9	46.3	44	1.2	0.2
1959	49.4	58	5.9	0.9	43.8	41	0.9	0.1
1964	43	43	11	1.4	44	50.3	5.3	0.1
1966	42	40	8.5	2	48	58	1.7	0.1
1970	46.4	52.5	7.5	1	43	45.5	3.2	1

From this data, could you criticise the British electoral system?

One system which attempts to provide each party with its 'fair share' of seats is proportional representation. The United Kingdom is the only country in Europe which does not use a form of proportional representation. Under proportional representation there are usually larger constituencies, each one of which returns several MPs. In each constituency, the number of MPs returned for each party depends on the number of votes cast.

Devise various ways of deciding how many MPs of each party should be returned in a multiple MP constituency. Which way of allocating MPs do you think is fairest?

2 OPTIMUM DESIGN

This project looks at the problem of designing an economic tin can. What factors do you think will affect the cost of a tin can? Use the modelling process to find the best shape of cylinder to hold a given volume. Compare your theoretical result with the shapes of actual tins. Try to refine your model.

3 A CAR CRASH

A car C was rounding a blind bend when the driver saw a van V in front. On realising that the van was stationary, the car driver hit the brakes. However, he skidded out of control on the wet road and collided with a car X, going the other way. Car C bounced off car X and crashed into the back of van V, causing considerable damage.

The driver of car C argues that the van was parked too close to the corner. The van driver argues that C was driving too fast. The driver of car X feels that she is an innocent party, so whose insurance company should she claim from?

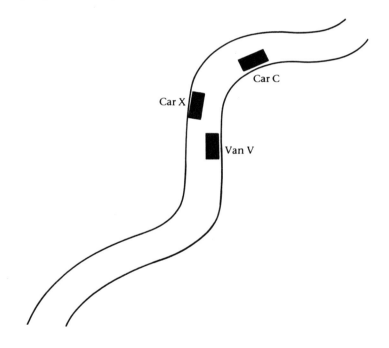

- Try to state the problem involved here mathematically.

- What factors do you consider important in this problem?

- Which variables do you think you should include in your model?

- If your first model proves too complex, can you simplify the problem at all by making some assumptions?

4 DOES THE CITY OF NEWCHESTER NEED A METRO?

Many of the city councillors in Newchester have noticed that other big cities in the country have metro 'light railway rapid transit' systems as part of their public transport service. They think it would be a symbol of prestige if their city had one too. However, other councillors argue that it is not needed and would be a waste of money.

Suppose you were called in as a consultant to advise on the need for a metro. How would you proceed?

5 RESALE VALUE OF A SECONDHAND CAR

It is well known that, in general, a car loses value. Two models have been proposed to predict the resale value of a car, £S, after time t years.

(a) $S = S_0 - kt$ (linear),

(b) $S = S_0 e^{-kt}$ (negative exponential),

where £S_0 is the value of the car when new, in each case.

Decide which of these models is preferable.

Criticise the models and suggest improvements.

6 FAMINE RELIEF

Your school is about to submit a petition to the World Health Organisation in Geneva for a global policy on famine relief. You decide to attempt a model solution to the problem to accompany the petition. What form does it take?

7 MAGAZINE SALES

A news kiosk is sited in the business quarter of a city, so its trade is not seasonal. There are some sales of confectionery, etc., but the main trade is in newspapers and magazines. The vendor's problem is that if he overstocks with a particular magazine he is left with copies on his hands; if he understocks then he loses dissatisfied customers. Those who buy magazines may also buy other items.

After consulting a newsagent (not in the rush hour!), devise a model to solve the vendor's problem and maximise his profit.

8 PETROL CONSUMPTION IN CARS

Construct a model relating rate of petrol consumption to as many relevant factors as possible – mass of car, engine capacity, speed, road conditions and so on – and check your model against data published by vehicle manufacturers.

9 SAVINGS

A friend inherits a lump sum and decides to make it the basis of a savings account, to be added to by monthly payments by standing order from the bank. He asks your advice about the relative merits of the various forms of saving available.

Advise him, setting up models to predict the value of his savings in ten years' time under various schemes. (Assume he is in regular employment.)

Solutions

1 Mathematical enquiries

1.1 Introduction

1

		Joe's way	Susan's way
(a)	byes	5	2
(b)	rounds	4	4
(c)	matches	10	10

Note that a player given a 'bye' in a round of a tournament is not required to play in that round but carries on to the next round.

The type of notation used can be an important aid in solving the problem. Joe's method of running the tournament could be illustrated like this.

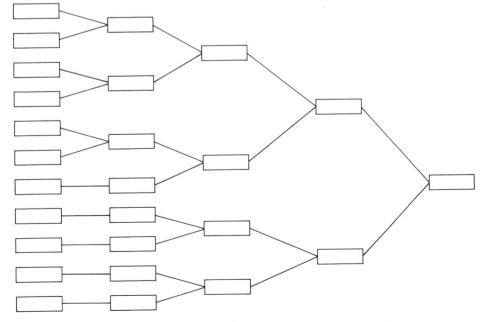

Are there any better ways of recording the investigation?

The number of matches played is always one less than the number of competitors. An amusingly brief proof of this can be given – everybody loses once except the winning finalist!

The number of byes is zero only if there are 2^n players.

For P players under Joe's system, the number of rounds is given by n where $2^{n-1} < P \le 2^n$. The number of byes is then $2^n - P$.

Under Susan's system there can be at most one bye per round. Can a more precise rule be discovered?

2   Differences formed from numbers with an odd number of digits are divisible by 99. Differences from numbers with an even number of digits are divisible by 9.

By looking at particular examples such as

$$365 = (3 \times 100) + (6 \times 10) + 5$$

you can see the general result that a number **looking like** ABC actually has the value $100A + 10B + C$. So the difference between this number and the one with digits reversed is

$$100A + 10B + C - (100C + 10B + A) = 99(A - C)$$

(You may have managed to give an explanation for these results without using algebra.)

One fruitful line of investigation concerns using 'differencing' to form chains of numbers. All chains from non-palindromic two-digit numbers end in the cycle:

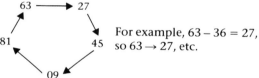

For example, $63 - 36 = 27$, so $63 \rightarrow 27$, etc.

What happens with three-digit numbers, four-digit numbers, . . .?

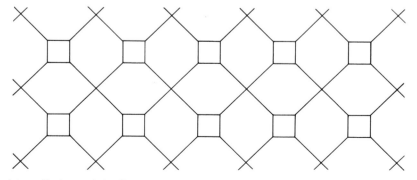

3   A tessellation originally was the result of covering an area with **tesserae**, the small square blocks used by the Romans to make mosaics. Nowadays, from the primary school onward, it is generally accepted as any covering or 'tiling' of a plane surface of indefinite extent by a regular pattern of one or more congruent non-overlapping shapes. For example:

(a) A parallelogram tessellation can be obtained from one for rectangles by a shear:

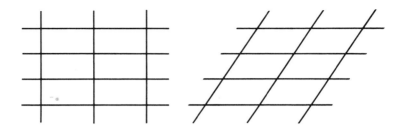

For extensions it might be more useful to think of the parallelograms forming strips which can then be fitted together easily.

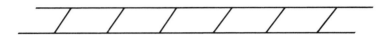

(b) Perhaps the most obvious method is to fit copies of the triangle together in pairs to form parallelograms

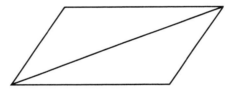

but finding other patterns might be a profitable exercise.

(c) The 108° corners cannot be fitted together to form 360° and so regular pentagons cannot tessellate.

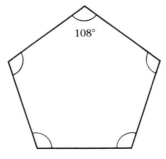

This idea might be used to establish the fact that only three regular shapes will tessellate on a plane surface – an equilateral triangle, a square and a regular hexagon.

Further extensions might include tackling questions such as the following:

Do all pentagons with one pair of parallel sides tessellate?

Are there any other pentagons which will tessellate?

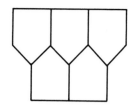

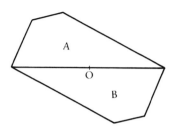

Quadrilateral B has been obtained from quadrilateral A by rotating it through 180° about O, the midpoint of a side. Repeated applications of this principle give a tessellation of quadrilaterals.

As an extension you could check that the method works for re-entrant quadrilaterals, such as

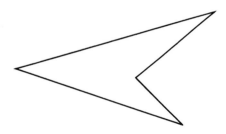

and explain **why** the method always works.

1.2   **Starting an enquiry**

> What general **pattern** is suggested by the numbers obtained on the right-hand side?

The numbers on the right-hand side are all squares (1^2), 3^2, 6^2, 10^2, . . .

> Can you refine the **pattern** so that there is some easy way of predicting what the square number will be for each particular case?

The squares on the right-hand sides are of

$$(1), 3, 6, 10, 15, 21, \ldots$$

and $(1 = 1)$

$$3 = 1 + 2$$
$$6 = 1 + 2 + 3$$
$$10 = 1 + 2 + 3 + 4$$

etc. You should expect (and you can check) that

$$1^3 + 2^3 + 3^3 + 4^3 + 5^3 + 6^3 + 7^3 = (1 + 2 + 3 + 4 + 5 + 6 + 7)^2$$

> Explain the **pattern** of the original results in words.

The sum of the cubes of the first n positive integers is equal to the square of the sum of those integers.

1.3   Particular cases

E X E R C I S E   2

1   If $a = 0$ then x is the cube root of $-b$.

If $b = 0$ then

$$x^3 + ax = 0$$
$$\Rightarrow x (x^2 + a) = 0$$
$$\Rightarrow x = 0 \text{ or } x^2 + a = 0$$

and further roots can be found only if $a < 0$.

2   The right-angled triangle might be a useful first example, since such a triangle is half a rectangle and since **any** triangle may be dissected into two right-angled triangles.

3 $x = 0$ (y is not defined)
x small and positive (y is large and positive)
x small and negative (y is large and negative)
x large (y is approximately equal to x)

4 Two such examples are:

(a) $a = 1$, $b = 2$, $c = 4$, $d = 3$, $e = 6$, $f = 7$

(b) $a = 1$, $b = 2$, $c = 4$, $d = 3$, $e = 6$, $f = 12$

Write out the equations with these coefficients to see why. You will also see that there is an infinity of possible answers.

1.4 Forming patterns

E X E R C I S E 3

1 $43\,681 = 209^2$. So, assuming that d is the greatest of a, b, c and d, $d = (n + 3)$ where

$$n^2 + 3n + 1 = 209$$

The numbers are 13, 14, 15 and 16.

2 The recurrence relation is

$$u_{n+2} = u_{n+1} + u_n$$

(a) 21, 34

(b) $8^2 = (13 \times 5) - 1$, $13^2 = (21 \times 8) + 1$, etc.

(c) The 4th, 8th and 12th terms are 3, 21 and 144. They are all multiples of 3.

(d) The 5th, 10th and 15th terms are all multiples of 5. Generally, every nth term is divisible by u_n.

1.5 Generalisation

E X E R C I S E 4

1 (a) $\displaystyle\sum_{i=1}^{n} (2i - 1) = n^2$

(b) The sum of the first n odd numbers is n^2.

2 (a) Divisible by 3; divisible by 8.

(b) The sum of n consecutive odd numbers is divisible by n if n is odd, and by $2n$ if n is even.

3 $2, 5, 9, \frac{1}{2}n(n-3)$

4 A polygon of given perimeter has greatest area if it is regular, i.e. all its angles are equal and all its sides are equal.

2 Organising your work

2.1 Notation and symbols

E X E R C I S E 1

1 R S L S S L

The route is shown in this grid.

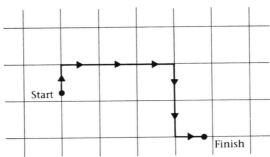

2 The cells could be labelled as shown. Alternatively a coordinate system could be used, indicating the row and column of the cell.

1	2	3
4	5	6
7	8	9

3 A similar statement is true for all such sets. Let the first number be n, then

$$n^2 + (n+3)^2 + (n+5)^2 + (n+6)^2 = (n+1)^2 + (n+2)^2 + (n+4)^2 + (n+7)^2$$

because both sides simplify to $4n^2 + 28n + 70$.

4   A simple pictorial notation might be ⌴ for an upright tumbler, and ⊓ for one which is upside down.

However, the explanation hinges on ideas of oddness and evenness (parity) and so a numerical notation is better.

Let 1 represent an upright tumbler and 0 one which is upside down. Start with a sum $1 + 0 + 1 = 2$, which is even. Because you change two at a time the sum will remain even, i.e. always be 0 or 2, and never 3 as required.

2.2   Classifying

E X E R C I S E   2

1   (a) Acute, right, obtuse, straight, reflex, . . .

(b) Scalene, isosceles, equilateral, right-angled, . . .

(c) Prisms, shapes having one curved surface, shapes having a plane of symmetry, . . .

2   Using the notation of question 2 of exercise 1, first moves in cells 1, 3, 7 and 9 are essentially alike, as are those in cells 2, 4, 6 and 8. There are therefore three essentially different first moves.

3   Rectangles and rhombi

4   The possible cases are:

- a and b both even, then $a^2 + b^2$ is a multiple of 4;

- one odd, one even, then $a^2 + b^2 = 4k + 1$ (see below);

- a and b both odd, then $a^2 + b^2 = 4k + 2$.

  If, for example,

  $$a = (2m + 1) \text{ and } b = 2n, \text{ then}$$
  $$a^2 + b^2 = 4m^2 + 4m + 1 + 4n^2$$
  $$= 4(m^2 + m + n^2) + 1$$
  $$= 4k + 1, \text{ say}$$

5   Is it shaded? Is it made up of straight lines (rectilinear)? Has it more than two lines of symmetry?

2.3   Tabulation

E X E R C I S E   3

1

n	3	4	5	6
$D(n)$	0	2	5	9

$D(n)$ is the number of diagonals of an *n*-gon.

A decagon has 35 diagonals.

2

Shape	No. of lines of symmetry	Order of rotational symmetry
Parallelogram	0	2
Rhombus	2	2
Rectangle	2	2
Kite	1	1
Square	4	4

3

n	1	2	3	4	5	6
$r(n)$	1	2	2	3	3	4
$s(n)$	1	2	3	5	8	13

$$r(n) = \begin{cases} \frac{1}{2}(n+1) & \text{if } n \text{ is odd} \\ \frac{1}{2}n + 1 & \text{if } n \text{ is even} \end{cases}$$

$s(n) = s(n-1) + s(n-2)$ for $n \geq 3$

with $s(1) = 1, s(2) = 2$

4 Completing investigations

4.1   Counter-example

E X E R C I S E   1

1 $x = -1, y = 0$ disproves the statement.

2   False. The three-dimensional cartesian axes are a counter-example.

3   False. 21 is the first counter-example.

4 $t_1 = 1$, $t_2 = 2$, $t_3 = 3$, $t_4 = 4$, $t_5 = 29$. The value of t_5 is **not** 5 as might be expected if you considered only the first four terms.

4.2 Proof

Verify that the L-shaped shells have areas 8, 27 and 64 square units respectively.

The fourth L-shaped shell has dimensions as shown.

The area is $(4 \times 6) + (4 \times 4) + (6 \times 4) = 64$. The areas of the other shells can similarly be checked.

Find areas A, B and C and show that $A + B + C = k^3$.

$A = k \times \frac{1}{2}k(k - 1) = \frac{1}{2}k^2(k - 1)$

$B = \frac{1}{2}k^2(k - 1)$

$C = k^2$

$A + B + C = \frac{1}{2}k^2(k - 1) + \frac{1}{2}k^2(k - 1) + k^2$

$\qquad\qquad = k^2(k - 1) + k^2 = k^3$

EXERCISE 2

1 In the 5×13 'rectangle' a very thin parallelogram of area 1 is missing.

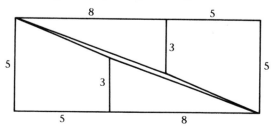

A 'similar triangles' argument shows this: $\frac{3}{8} \neq \frac{5}{13}$

2   In the product $n \times (n - 3)$, each diagonal is counted twice. There are therefore $\frac{1}{2}n(n - 3)$ diagonals.

3   (a)   The numbers may in general be written as $(2a - 1)$ and $(2a + 1)$, with sum $4a$.

(b)   The sum of the numbers may be written as

$$(2a + 1) + (2a + 3) + (2a + 5) + \ldots + (2a + 2n - 1)$$
$$= (2a + 2a + 2a + 2a + \ldots + 2a) + (1 + 3 + 5 + \ldots + 2n - 1)$$
$$= 2na + n^2$$
$$= n(2a + n)$$

This expression is divisible by n. For n even, it is divisible by 2.

5 Mathematical articles

5.2   Reading mathematics

EXERCISE   1   (QUESTION   1)

(*1)   At this stage you should draw a few doodles such that your pen comes back to its starting point each time. For example:

 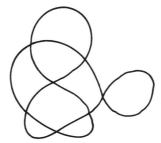 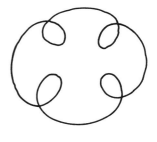

When the author of the article makes definitions about such graphs you can then use your own drawings as illustrations.

At this point you would probably read on a few lines to check that the author is going to define the phrase '4-regular'.

(*2) Each of the author's definitions and statements should be checked:

(a) Number of crossing points, $n = 9$.
(b) Number of edges, $m = 18$.
(c) Number of regions, $r = 11$.
(d) 34589 defines the shaded region.
(e) There is a region exterior to the graph!

(a, b, c) For the doodles given in answer to question 1:

$n = 1$	$n = 7$	$n = 4$
$m = 2$	$m = 14$	$m = 8$
$r = 3$	$r = 9$	$r = 6$

(d,e) The region exterior to the graph of figure 1 is defined by 167892.

(*3) It could be argued that in the doodle

the only crossing point has **2** edges adjoined to it. In fact, mathematicians would still count this figure-of-eight doodle as 4-regular. One simple way to prevent the doodle being 4-regular is to retrace the path at some point, for example,

(*4) To answer this you must be clear about precisely what is allowable as a 'doodle'.

In fact, it is a result of graph theory that **any** connected 4-regular graph can be drawn without retracing your path or lifting your pen off the paper.

(A graph such as is 4-regular but **disconnected**.)

(*5) The assertions should be checked on the doodle of figure 1. The values of k for the k-gons are shown below:

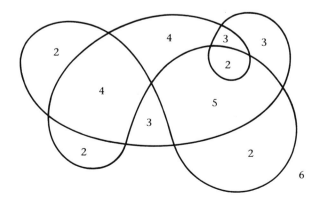